82 218

HQ
777.4   Knight, Bryan M.
.K5
           Enjoying single
           parenthood

DATE DUE

JY 1 '82	SE 30 '92		
JA 3 '84			
OC 16 '85	NO 30 '92		
AP 18 '86	SE 28 '94		
JY 23 '87			
MY 22 '89			
JE 5 '89			
AP 30 '90			
JY 29 '91			
MY 4 '92			
MY 29 '92			

enjoying
SINGLE PARENTHOOD

BRYAN M. KNIGHT, M.S.W.

VAN NOSTRAND REINHOLD LTD., *Toronto,*
New York, Cincinnati, London, Melbourne

Published simultaneously in the United
States of America by Van Nostrand
Reinhold Company, New York

Library of Congress Catalogue Number
80-50577

CANADIAN CATALOGUING IN PUBLICATION DATA
Knight, Bryan M., 1939-
    Enjoying single parenthood

ISBN 0-442-29623-1

1. Single parents. 2. Single-parent family.
I. Title.

HQ777.4.K55   362.8'2   C80-094627-8

Editorial Consultant: Sandra Gulland/Words &
Design: Brant Cowie/Artplus Ltd.
Cover Photographs: Paterson Photographic Works
Typesetting: Dimensions in DesignType Ltd.
Printing and Binding: Webcom Limited
Printed and Bound in Canada

80 81 82 83 84 85 86 7 6 5 4 3 2 1

To E.M. and J.P., two vastly different women
to each of whom I owe an immense debt:
one for saving my mind,
the other for raising my morale,

and to my adorable children,
Angèle and Adrian

CONTENTS

PREFACE   v

ONE

On Your Own but Not Alone   1

TWO

Feel Fine, Feel Free   13

THREE

Overcome Loneliness   33

FOUR

A Time to Dream, a Time to Do   44

FIVE

Cut Expenses, Eat Well and Control Chores   57

SIX

Fight Prejudice and Discrimination   67

SEVEN

Sex and the Single Parent   94

EIGHT

Children: Extra Special People   116

RESOURCES   148

SUGGESTIONS FOR FURTHER READING   161

QUESTIONNAIRE   166

INDEX   168

Other books by Bryan M. Knight

Expropriation '67
The People Paradox (co-authored with Elisa Mion)
Fascinating History of Chess Pieces
Howard Staunton: Uncrowned Chess Champion of the World
The Laughter Book (co-authored with Doug Long)

Preface

I HAVE BEEN A SINGLE FATHER for nine years. My daughter is fifteen years old and my son is ten. Their mother and I decided to become legally separated for many reasons, not the least of which was that we thought it better for the children that we live apart. The children stay with their mother weekends and holidays. She is actively involved in their upbringing and both of us make sure the children visit grandparents and other family on both sides as frequently as possible.

The idea for this book was born out of reaction to the negative stereotypes of single parents I encountered everywhere. The amazement of people at my "being able to manage" irked me. Also, the more I enjoyed being a single parent—and met others also relishing their role--the more I thought a practical book expounding the positive aspects of single parenthood should be written.

This book is for all single parents: male and female, never-married, separated, divorced or widowed. It weaves together my own opinions and experiences and those of about a hundred other single parents. Thirty or so single parents were interviewed at length and in person in various cities and small towns. Most of these interviews were with single mothers. Some—like those taking a course for which I was a resource person—were managing on low incomes. Others had medium- or well-paying occupations. Another two dozen single mothers and fathers wrote or sent tape recordings to me as a result of two appeals on the Canadian Broadcasting Company's program, "As It Happens." Some of those already mentioned plus another half a dozen single parents answered a lengthy, open-ended questionnaire which I devised (a shortened version is shown on page 166). The questionnaire was distributed by mail and through acquaintances. I have also used material from my interviews with single mothers and fathers that formed the basis for two series of articles in a metropolitan newspaper. Several other single parents examined the manuscript at various stages and offered suggestions and anecdotes for its improvement. Finally, the comments of children interviewed individually and in groups have enriched me and the book.

All single parents are quoted under pseudonyms and sometimes with other details altered because some might be in legally vulnerable positions and because I guaranteed confidentiality to anyone kind enough to answer the questionnaire, be interviewed, write letters or send tapes.

To get the most out of this volume you need a pencil. Not just for noting your comments in the margins but for the charts. These work sheets are for your own use; no one else need see them. They are intended to prod your thinking and self-evaluation, to help you define your own guidelines and to encourage you to achieve your goals.

You will *not* find a roundup of opinions and theories from psychiatrists, doctors, social workers or psychologists in the following pages. The experts quoted are single parents who understand your situation. Man or woman, Ph.D. or grade-school graduate, young or old, one child or nine, these single parents invite you — through the synthesis of their experience — to enjoy single parenthood.

Many thanks to all the single parents who contributed to this book. And a special thank you to Laurie Coulter, Trade Editor of Van Nostrand Reinhold, for her unflagging enthusiasm from the beginning, and Sandra Gulland, for her excellent editing.

ONE

ON YOUR OWN
BUT NOT ALONE

SINGLE PARENTHOOD CAN BE A POSITIVE LIFE-STYLE for both parent and child. Nearly 20 percent of North American families are headed by one parent. That's more than half a million in Canada and nine million in the United States.

Among these families are many who thoroughly enjoy their single-parent status. Happy single parents enjoy their children. They also relish their freedom. Typical of this feeling is Louise, a divorced mother with two teen-age sons:

I like being able to get up in the morning whenever I want to without worrying about disturbing my husband. I like keeping my own hours. I like not having to cater to what a man wants to do or what he wants to eat or whenever he wants to watch television. I like not having to make joint decisions about how you're going to spend your time, entertain your friends. Having more autonomy in all these areas is very satisfying.

Single parents are free to develop many kinds of adult relationships. Most married people are restricted—by custom, belief or guilt—in the nature and number of extra-marital (not necessarily sexual) relationships they feel they can pursue. Not so the single parent. This wider range of possibilities can benefit the child in a one-parent family.

Other advantages for a child growing up in a single-parent family include living according to one standard of discipline, receiving deeper attention from the parent, being encouraged to be self-reliant, being less dominated by adults and learning to live more sensitively and more tolerantly.

As the number of single-parent families grows, so does acceptance. Books, movies, newspapers, magazines and television increasingly reflect our existence, and are doing it more and more positively. Single mothers are portrayed as competent and single fathers as compassionate.

Many single parents who have grown to enjoy the new life-style have conquered numerous setbacks. The emotional upheaval of separation, divorce, death of a spouse or unwed parenthood can be a spur to deeper self-knowledge and more positive living.

Here's what four single parents—all now enjoying single parenthood—have to say. Pat, a mother of three preteen girls:

When I asked my husband to leave our home, this decision was both destructive of my former life and constructive for myself and the girls' future. I had always believed myself unattractive, incompetent and incapable of inspiring affection. Where I stand now gives me a greater understanding of the enormous improvements that can be wrought in people when they are committed to change.

Ken, shy young father of Daniel:

I've become a much stronger person. Much more outgoing, much more willing to articulate my own feelings, my own views. I'm much less suppressed and intimidated by other people.

Melissa, a thirty-year-old never-married mother says with a smile:

I enjoy my daughter's company; I like her as a person. Single parents are no different from other parents in their love and enjoyment of children, but we do face different challenges and opportunities. Sole responsibility is an example. I find it easier to make decisions alone: it gives me a good feeling of accomplishment to carry all the responsibility.

Nina is raising nine children by herself:

The separated or divorced single parent will find the first six months to a year the loneliest and hardest. Once a routine is established and the new home begins to feel like home, the pressure diminishes. As time goes by, the parent begins to see happy changes in the children that prove that the new environment is beneficial. Life progressively gets better.

I say this because I have been through an experience that was packed full of problems and I am now living a much more balanced, happy life.

CHALLENGING
SEXUAL STEREOTYPES

Single parents find that their innovative role arouses anxiety in other people. Comments such as, "You make a good mother," said half in jest, half accusingly to the single father are common. It is as though, on the one hand, a man should not be capable of parenting well because he is a man and, on the other, he is disturbing people's sexual identity by undertaking hitherto "women's work." Similarly, the determination a single mother must show to earn enough to support her children can cause her to be called "an aggressive bitch," presumably because she is displaying a toughness only acceptable in males.

Everyone has masculine and feminine qualities. Since one or the other part is usually suppressed, the overt behavior of single fathers will sometimes disconcert other people, particularly men. It takes a single father comfortable with himself and his masculinity not to feel awkward in the face of such embarrassment, especially when he dons an apron to do dishes. Equally, a single mother must have confidence in her femininity when male co-workers sneer as she clamps a hard hat on her head.

Another prejudice claims that every child needs a mother and a father. Actually, there is no magic element in either that makes the father or the mother an essential parent. Biologically, yes, but after that a man or a woman alone is equally capable of raising a child well. On their own, they might even do a better job.

Except for some never-married parents, single parenthood is largely a found, rather than a chosen, state. Choice rests only on the question of remaining a single parent, and how best to fulfill the challenge.

Some single parents cannot see how similar their situation is to other single parents. One will think because he became a single parent through the death of his wife he has little in common with the divorcée, who in turn may consider that she is quite different from the never-married single parent. All are overlooking the emotional processes, the child-rearing tasks, the practical discriminations and the joys of single parenthood, which are essentially similar for all of them.

SEPARATED
SINGLE PARENTS

The separated single parent goes through a period of mixed feelings at the beginning of the unfamiliar role. There is often a sense of relief, mixed with hurt and resentment. The feeling of freedom eventually triumphs over wounded pride and the sense of loss.

Much of the sense of loss arises from the absence of familiar patterns of behavior. Even when these were full of conflict, they were predictable. And even though their very predictability was often one of the sore points between a husband and wife, the suddeness of no longer having them is disconcerting. The shock of adaptation to the new life-style can be beneficial. The single parent is forced into self reappraisal but is also freer to pursue his or her own desires without the hindrance—real or imagined—of a spouse.

Separated parents form about 20 percent of single parents, and even those whose separation was relatively friendly face emotional upheaval. Desertion creates more of a shock than does deliberate separation for the well-being of the child or the expulsion of the other parent. Most separated single parents take a year or more to resolve their inner emotional storms.

DIVORCED
SINGLE PARENTS

Almost a third of all single parents have been divorced. The emotional effects of divorce vary. Sometimes divorce is merely an official acknowledgement of the long-time absence of one partner; sometimes it is a mutually agreed upon decision with little bitterness; more frequently, divorce is the end result of antagonism between people who once had a high regard for each other. Under our present legal system, this discord is often fanned by lawyers, to the detriment of the children.

Most divorced single parents have to face a situation common to many in the separated category but to only a few in the never-married and none in the widowed: the other parent is a physical, as well as an emotional, reality.

WIDOWED
SINGLE PARENTS

Nearly 30 percent of single parents are widowed. More than three-quarters of them are women. In popular mythology, the widowed are likely to be accorded more sympathy and acceptance. Such support is often short-lived and the challenges of single parenthood are the same as for all other categories. The challenges are compounded by the single parent's having to come to terms with the death of the partner-parent. Grief and guilt may or may not be mixed with the emotions of relief, resentment, anger and separation anxiety common to the other categories of single parenthood.

NEVER-MARRIED
SINGLE PARENTS

Never-married single parents include single persons who adopted, gave birth to, fathered or accepted a child as a ward, but who have never married. (A divorcée could give birth and would technically be an unmarried mother but not, by definition, a never-married mother.)

Never-married single parents form about 20 percent of all single parents. The number of single people who have adopted children is likely to be very small, given the comparatively low total of never-married single parents, the preference of adoption workers in social agencies for two-parent families and the current shortage of children available for adoption.

The single parent by adoption tends, because of social pressure and life circumstance, to be older and wealthier than the average never-married mother who bears and rears her own child. Of the minority of singles who have adopted, even fewer are men. This is not surprising considering society's emphasis on nurturing as a woman's task. Adoptive single parents are more likely , because of "market" conditions, to parent mixed-race or handicapped and older children. They also tend to have three or four children. Most mothers bearing their own tend to have only one or at the most three children.

The adopting single parent has made a positive, definitive, conscious choice to enhance his or her single state. While there usually has to be a determined effort and a lengthy wait for the child, this anxiety is different from that of the never-married woman bearing her own child. Rarely is the decision to become pregnant and keep the baby a conscious, determined act. Most of the mothers interviewed had discovered that they were pregnant and then decided to keep the child. Sometimes the decision was swift. Other women made up their minds after the baby was born. In all cases, of course, these single mothers, unlike their adopting counterparts, experienced childbirth, the early years of babyhood and day-care dilemmas:

I felt I had a responsibility to my unborn child. I made the decision to accept that responsibility. I felt capable of raising her, though I knew at times it might not be easy. But I was determined. I wouldn't let myself be overwhelmed by all the talk about how my baby would have problems because she had no father, and I've been proven right; it's not true at all. My daughter's ten now, and we've had a good life together. I'm puzzled by people who ask, "Wasn't it difficult?"

And a single woman who adopted three children explains:

I suppose I've always liked children. I quickly rejected the idea of bearing illegitimate children because it would mean time off work and young babies and a certain social stigma. And for me there would be an emotional problem, too. I would like to be in love with the children's father, and if I was in love with him, I'd prefer to be attached to him.

For various reasons I didn't think of adopting earlier. I had to fight to get these children. The agency at first said I was ineligible because I was single and working; later they said there were no kids. I knew this was not true and the other points were ridiculous. So I fought. I pestered the agency with phone calls.

I've had the first child three and a half years and the two boys a year; it's our anniversary next week. I can't understand why people regard being a single parent as such a burden, why it has to be such a terrible crisis. People ask me, "Don't you find it hard to deal with problems on your own?" Well, basically, no I don't, because I'm used to dealing with problems on my own and I find that people are very kind.

I wanted the children. I wasn't in the position where I had them and suddenly found I was stuck with the children without a partner. I've never wished I didn't have them, even though I get very angry at times and I'll yell and shout. There are days when I just feel I've got to get out. This is normal I think. But I've never thought I can't stand the next eight or ten years till they're out from under my feet.

SINGLE
FATHERS

The increase in single parenthood, and single fatherhood in particular, is a social phenomenon, although it may appear to the individual father to be simply a personal situation. Changes in attitudes toward marriage and the family are part of much wider changes in society at large. Single fatherhood is one indicator of these broader changes. It is on the increase largely because of the new status of women. Employment of women has gone beyond the wartime mentality of women filling in for fighting men. Women are increasingly career-oriented. As financial possibilities change, so do expectations and practices. Wives, no longer totally dependent financially on their husbands, have found it easier to leave:

Women say, "How could she leave?" I find myself defending my wife having the courage to at least decide to leave rather than sticking around and making it kind of miserable for everybody. She had to have a certain amount of courage to make that decision, especially in the face of her family pressures. She made the decision and left, and that's fine. We split while we were still on an amiable basis rather than the whole affair degenerating into throwing insults or plates or something.

As this form of equality has grown, so it has become more acceptable to more mothers. Now when a wife feels trapped and unfulfilled, it is no longer so shocking for her to strike out on her own.

A consequence of the changes in women's roles has been new expectations of those of men. Fathers find it more acceptable, even desirable, to care for their children on their own. More men are less hesitant to accept custody or to fight for it. Even where legal custody is not possible, men are increasingly accepting so-called "open custody": the mother has legal custody but the children live with the father. And joint custody—maintaining both parents' rights and responsibilities for the children, which usually results in the father's having equal time with the children—is gaining in popularity.

Other factors include geographical mobility and the increased diffusion of the family away from other kin. The importance of all these changes is that men can more and more feel free to enjoy single fatherhood:

Women say it's not natural to see a man bathing children and doing this and doing that. But it's women who make those comments, not men, for some peculiar reason. They're more chauvinistic about parental duties than the men are. Male friends of mine take it for granted; I have the children and I do what has to be done. But when they visit, their wives say, "Oh it's awful to see you with your sleeves rolled up bathing kids."

The single father is relatively new in our society. There are no generally accepted ways of behaving toward single fathers. Attitudes vary from ostracism to sympathy, from wonderment to disapproval, depending, partly, on the reason for the father's being single:

One big advantage in being a single father as opposed to being a single mother is that I get much more sympathy than they do. Society takes it for granted if there's a marriage breakup that mummy keeps the kids. So people are sorry for them, but not unduly sorry because they're a fairly large group, whereas single dads are still unique enough to most of the people I know that I get an extraordinary amount of sympathy. That doesn't actually translate itself into physical help very much, but at least people are kind of nice about it. Well, you're such a good chap and you're such a martyr and you're doing so much for your children. In fact I vainly tell them that the children do a lot for me, too, and that I get a terrific kick out of being with them and having all the funny little experiences you have with children aged four, five and six.

The issue of work is an example of the uncertainty of public attitudes toward single fathers. While many people consider that a mother can happily, indeed even *should,* stay home with her child, no such freedom of choice is awarded to single fathers. The adage that "a woman's place is in the home" implies that a man's place is *out* of the home. Thus state support of a single father who would like to remain home with his child is frowned upon. Similarly, when a man puts his child before his career, he is considered either weird, courageous or stupid:

I gave up what is known as a "promising career" as a radio broadcaster and got a job in a delicatessen so I'd have no conflicts about overtime or weekend work. Now I can be with my daughter much more, and regularly. I want to be clear that nothing I've done was unselfish. I changed my work and life-style because my daughter is the greatest. I enjoy being with her, I love her. It's all selfishness on my part.

Johnny is twenty-seven, the father of two. His enjoyment of single parenthood is not unusual:

I have been raising the children for quite a while now, and mostly it's great. Andrew will be five soon and starting kindergarten in a month. Tina just turned three.

The house we are living in is quite old and small so I have decided to build a new one, all myself. I drew up the plans, did the excavating, and started right in. The kids spend a lot of their time playing around the new house and they have learned the names and uses of all the tools and can identify various pieces of lumber, nails, shingles, etc. It's amazing how easily they pick these things up. Andrew is old enough to be a little "go-for" for me now and then and can do the odd small job to help. Tina just pounds nails in various undesired places and generally slows things down a little but that's okay because I've got lots of time.

When I'm not building my house, I'm farming. Since I only operate a grain farm, I will have all winter to do exactly as I please. I have been considering taking the kids in a camper down to Mexico for about a month or so during the worst of winter, probably during January.

My kids have been doing very well through the separation. They play together a lot and they have a number of good friends in town. Andrew has just learned how to ride a two-wheeler so now Tina gets left behind more while he goes riding around with friends, but she doesn't usually mind too much. I take them with me as much as I can and they spend many days riding around in old trucks hauling grain, or watching me work on machinery.

Haung, a thirty-three-year-old single father of a five-year-old girl, used to be anxious about parenting. He has been a single father for three years following his wife's departure.

When Kate was born, I really didn't know her at all for the first eight or nine months. When Joan and I were going to break up, we had long discussions about me keeping the baby. I won because I could offer income and a stable environment. Joan wanted to travel. Joan took off because the baby was inhibiting her growth and I was belligerent about her smartening up. I was a typical male chauvinist pig. I believed in the traditional roles: she had her place. I was extremely hard on her. We're both much happier and more fulfilled now.

When Joan decided to go, I realized I really wanted to have the baby and not lose her. If I didn't take her, the odds were I wouldn't ever have gotten close to her.

I had to learn diapering and cooking. I didn't know what I was doing, but eventually I learned. I started to enjoy it. Every day it's a joy to take care of her, being with her, helping her grow up—a phenomenal experience. She's fascinating, and easy to take care of. I take her most places with me. Kate is a remarkable child. She has an excellent way of handling herself. At times she takes on adult characteristics but not in an obnoxious way.

By and large, single fatherhood is enjoyable, but I would rather be more active than I am. I don't like to work late, for example, because then I miss the baby. I don't want to get involved with emotional hang-ups or tie-ups. Marriage was so restricting and I couldn't do what I wanted, but now even with the kid, I'm doing more than then. But there are times when I come home from work and put the baby to bed and say, "Oh, shit, what a way to spend an evening." I even think maybe I should be married again, but this is only an odd occurrence when I'm tired or under particular strain at work.

A girl gains a lot from a close relationship with her single father. She sees him doing the housework; she's brought up in a nonsexist way so she grows up well-rounded and with greater ability to do the things she wants to do.

THE REWARDS
OF SINGLE PARENTING

The most important aspect of single parenthood is surely the relationship between parent and child. Most single parents really enjoy their children and develop close ties with them. The parents are warm and competent. Abe, a single father of two, claims "there is a better relationship between kids and their single dad. My boys, for instance, are more responsible. They're part of this family unit." When a child expresses his affection, in words or gestures, it does wonders for a single parent:

One day I was feeling very down. My little son came up on my lap, looked at me with his big brown eyes, and stroked my head with his tiny hand. I gave him a big hug because he had reminded me how lucky I am to be a single father. A few minutes later, he was shouting and thumping around as usual.

Children have a built-in tolerance for the peculiarities of a single parent. They may not be able to articulate their love, but it's there. In a way, this is the driving force for a single parent to live positively, no matter how hurt and depressed he or she may be at the outset. A powerful sense of purpose is instilled in a single parent by a determination to make sure the child suffers as little as possible from the absence of another parent.

Bill raised his son alone for three years after his wife walked out on him and the newborn baby. Bill's second wife—the only mother Justin knew—had been gone two months when Bill said:

My son is taking it very, very hard. He's afraid I'll leave him too. When I was a single father for three years, although it was emotionally difficult the job was pretty simple. With a child this age, the job is not so simple. He's going through a stage now of getting into trouble to test me. "You will get angry and leave me." "No, I won't. Even though I get angry, I still love you and I won't leave."

One of the major benefits a single parent receives is deeper communication with his or her child and the maturity to express and acknowledge feelings. A single father cannot remain locked for long in the "tough man, me-never-cry" role. Antoine speaks for many single fathers when he says:

I hardly ever talked to my children about feelings and emotions. Since the separation, we discuss a lot together about how we feel; now we're all much closer.

A single woman with two girls and two boys agrees:

I feel you have to share your emotions with your children to some extent. If I'm tired, I'll tell them I want to lie down for half an hour, then I'll be all right. "It's not your fault, I just need to rest a while." If I'm really upset about something and sit down and cry, I explain that I was tired tonight and, "When you broke those glasses on the floor, that was the last straw and now I'm crying but afterward I'll feel better." And after I will say, "Yes, I do feel better, I've had a cry and we'll put the whole thing behind us." Children have to realize you're human too. You can feel bad and you can get over it.

More than twelve million children under eighteen in Canada and the United States have parents that are divorced. Every year an-

other million children join them. Those whose parents do not immediately remarry, join the hordes of other single-parent families—
divorced, separated, widowed or never-married. Each of these families decides to concentrate on calamity or to defy dilemmas.
Among those who chose to enjoy single parenthood are the following parents:

I'm constantly learning and changing along with the children. Maybe
that's the answer.

If one is open, the changes aren't so dramatic or traumatic. I've gone
from infancy to preteen; highs and lows; I could have felt like a prisoner, a
maid, a drudge, etc., (and have at moments felt all that) but I made choices
—I chose to bear children, chose to divorce, chose to be alone and, so, I
must also choose to be responsible for the situation that I am in.

That is my reality, and surely it is a joy to be alive, with healthy children, doing good work, here and now.

One advantage is that I'm not trying to share myself between a husband
and the children. I'm not saying I'm against men, it's not that at all. But
since this is the position, I think it is an advantage. The children know exactly where they stand; they can't play me off against anybody. There's no
conflict about what discipline they will have. There's no trying to divide
myself in two. An advantage of being a single person is that you can chart
your life, plan where you're going without having to worry about a
partner.

I'm very proud of the special closeness I have with my girls and I would not
have had that special relationship if I had been sharing them all the time
with their mother.

I enjoy doing things with the children. I love seeing them grow up and I
enjoy their company and we can have a lot of fun together. I think I like
children's fresh view of things. We go places—zoos, parks, movies, ballet
—we garden together, swim together, they come shopping with me. It's
fun to take one or two of them downtown with me. Or to take a particular
child to a lunch he or she will enjoy.

I really enjoy the pleasure of seeing Mark with the dog; it is his first.
Mark even puts his arms around it for comfort when he's in trouble. An-
other reward was the children's pleasure when we went to see *Nutcracker
Suite*. And seeing Theresa's face when we went to a flower show one day.
It was wintry outside. My daughter just stopped in the doorway, abso-
lutely incredulous. I realized that she'd never seen a blaze of color like that.
Those are the things that are fun. And after Christmas when Peter said to
me, "It's the best Christmas we've ever had, isn't it?" very spontaneously.
Yes, those are the little things that make it all completely worthwhile.

TWO

FEEL FINE
FEEL FREE

MANY OF US BEGIN SINGLE PARENTHOOD feeling worthless and bitter. Drained by months of marital conflict, stunned by the death of a spouse or dismayed by the responsibility of an illegitimate birth, we ask, "Why me?" Fear of being overwhelmed mingles with anger and guilt. Rejection—by spouse, friends or society—makes us feel inadequate. How will we possibly cope?

STOP
BLAMING YOURSELF

Feelings of guilt and shame are real for too many single parents. Sydney, a single father of ten-year-old Wayne and fifteen-year-old Sally, confesses:

I used to feel everything that went wrong was my fault. When Wayne had problems at school I blamed myself and the separation. Gradually, it became clear to me that I could only be one parent. This realization seems obvious now, but it was a great relief to me then. The children understood and everything became a lot easier for all of us.

The boy's school problems could have been caused by a personality clash with a teacher, eating certain foods or by poor eyesight. There could be many reasons. Don't assume that all your child's troubles are linked to his one-parent family status.

EMPATHY
EXERCISE

Here's a method for understanding how your child may feel sometimes. The exercise should also remind you that many of the things we blame ourselves for are actually caused by outside factors.

Think back to your own childhood. Think hard. Jot down the earliest incident you can recall in which you felt helpless, humiliated. It will most likely involve someone's laughing or sneering at you—someone bigger or smarter.

Close your eyes and picture yourself back in the scene. If you have a tape recorder, talk your story—complete with your feelings —into the machine. (Speak out loud as you write if you don't have a tape recorder.) Let your feelings flow; yield to your sorrow: cry, scream or bang your fists on the floor if you want.

Repeat the same procedure for two other incidents.

What did you learn? You may be surprised that pain you thought long forgotten could come back, but you should feel relief now that you have got it out. You will find that you empathize more readily with your child when she suffers. You'll be less likely to accept shame and guilt as automatically deserved. And, perhaps most important, you have proof that she will survive emotional upsets— after all, you did.

GET OVER
GUILT

Do you feel guilty because your child has "only" one parent? Many single parents torture themselves with feelings of blame. "If only I'd. . . " is a futile, plaintive introduction to harmful fantasies. You have to live in the present and accept the consequences of the past. One single father, who had a bitter fight to gain custody of his children, said his parents still try to play on his guilt:

"Your poor children." "You ruined your life." "What will people say?" It's a routine I've heard so often it's lost its impact. I no longer feel the need to justify myself, so I just kind of let them talk it out and then do what I like.

A divorced mother speaks more forcefully about guilt feelings:

The woman newly on her own must avoid feeling guilty and avoid overcompensating to her children—making up to them for the terrible crime she's committed. Baloney. When I think of my kids and the tension and their seeing me in tears and being beaten and whatever, how could I say that that was a better atmosphere than what they've got now?

Sure, I've got my ups and downs—but they're mine. And the kids have a far better relationship with their father now than then; before he couldn't even be bothered to spend one hour a week with them. So there should be no guilt feelings. The idea is to stop wallowing in self-pity and start doing something for yourself.

You don't have to suffer unnecessary guilt. If something that genuinely troubles your conscience needs to be atoned for, apologize, make restitution, act in a suitable way to cut off the cause of your guilt. But don't confuse such guilt-causers with your single-parent status. Don't condemn yourself for something beyond your control, such as your ex's indifference, brutality, alcoholism or infidelity.

If you are *certain* that you share some of the responsibility for your ex's behavior, then forgive yourself. Tell yourself, "That's in the past, it's done, I can't undo it. But I can do my best now—guilt-free—for the sake of my child."

There's no need to feel guilty because your child doesn't have both a mother and a father. You can't be both. Accept that. Stop punishing yourself for the impossible. You can't be father and mother and you don't need to be: you can be parent. (And if your mate is not permanently gone, encourage him or her to parent, too.)

Freeing oneself from guilt means adopting new standards. Why judge yourself by values that apply to a two-parent society?

Single mothers who had never been married used to be made to feel guilt and shame. Fortunately, attitudes are changing. This is reflected in one never-married mother's view of herself:

Am I supposed to feel guilty about something? If I'm supposed to feel guilty about having an illegitimate child, there's just no way; I simply don't. I remember my doctor asking me once during my first trimester of pregnancy if I respected myself. At the time I thought it was kind of a strange question. I didn't have any feelings of guilt or shame because I was pregnant; I was mostly concerned about the child, my future and if I had any kind of a future with the child's father.

Freda is another guilt-free never-married mother. By facing the world openly and with determination, she and hundreds like her are helping to bring about change. Change that means more options for her daughter:

Barbara can go into careers that formerly only men went into. She has the choice of marrying or not, or having children or not. She doesn't have to do these things anymore because it's expected of her. And if my daughter doesn't marry, she could still decide to have a child.

GUILT
EXERCISE

In the first column on the Guilt Chart, list everything you can think of that makes you feel guilty. In the second column—after thinking seriously about it—explain why you are or are not to blame. In the third column list what you are going to do, either to assuage deserved guilt or to shake off undeserved guilt.

DEFEAT
DEPRESSION

Depressed? Here's what to do—take your pick: wallow, weigh, speak or stretch.

Wallow in your depression and savor every moment like a glutton in an eating contest. Let yourself feel as miserable as possible; tell yourself all the horrible things you can think of to deepen your depression. See everything in a thoroughly pessimistic way and add even more gloom to the picture. Let the waves of self-pity flow freely. Keep this up for a while and you'll be laughing at your own exaggerations within the hour.

Weigh the reason for your sadness. Is the cause physical? Male single parents as well as female have cycles of feeling low. Maybe you are emotionally exhausted. Or constipated. Perhaps the cause is chemical. Too much to eat or drink? Too little? Missing your ex? Or sex? If your depression comes from any of these, the solution lies in the problem.

Speak and you can often resolve a mild depression. Talk to your cleric, friend, counselor or crisis line. Don't dump on dependents.

Stretch yourself. Instead of wallowing in misery, rooting out the cause or talking depression away, act. You might pray, go for a run, wash dishes, write a letter, sing a song or play ball with your child—anything as long as you're doing and not brooding. This technique may resolve the depression or postpone it (if the cause is something you can't face today).

Depression can't be drugged. Popping pills or abusing alcohol will only make things worse. At best, drugs provide a temporary illusion of well-being. The leg up is not worth the letdown.

FREE YOURSELF
FROM THE PAST

Many single parents are carrying a crushing load of anger toward or fear of their ex-partners. Their outlook on the world is based on what the ex did, would want, might like or hate. Sometimes the negative aspects of the ex are even seen by the single parent to be appearing in the child. Successful and happy single parenting begins with overcoming such destructive emotions.

It is hard to let go of another person. It is even harder to let go of your emotions, particularly when they run deep, as love and hurt usually do. Yet what is the alternative? Bitterness that eats away inside and thwarts whatever good intentions you might have in raising your child.

How do you let go of such destructive attitudes? First you must want to be rid of them. Then forgive yourself, gain perspective and deliberately forgive the other person's hurtful actions.

Crying is a natural way to release tension and shed distress. There is a period of "mourning" after any separation, any loss of another human being, even if that person is not dead or the emotional ties were not of love. The amount of time required for mourning differs from one individual to another.

Overcoming grief is not something you can program easily; nature has its own timetable. You must cooperate with the normal healing process. One single mother expected that a year would be a long enough time to mourn:

A year after the breakup I went through two or three really bad months because I thought a year marked the anniversary, and from that point forward I should begin to be more positive and happier and more together.

Some single parents discuss their distress with anyone, and everyone. Others are reluctant to talk at all about their feelings. Thirty-two-year-old Sonia was one of the quiet ones. An editor for a large

GUILT
CHART

I FEEL GUILTY ABOUT . . .	REASONS IT'S MY FAULT/NOT MY FAULT

GUILT
CHART

WHAT I INTEND TO DO ABOUT IT:

East Coast publisher, Sonia felt humiliated, resentful and badly hurt by her husband, who had gone off with her "best friend." For months, Sonia brooded and sulked, becoming more and more depressed. Her two daughters were frequently "bitchy at home and in trouble at school."

One night, I sat down and wrote till my hand ached. I poured out all my feelings, my bewilderment, my hurt, my anger, my fear, my resentment, my hatred.

At the end of this outpouring, I cried. I sat at the kitchen table where I had been writing and tears flooded onto the notepaper. After a while, I stopped sobbing. I found that the writing and the crying had relaxed a lot of the pent-up tension. I slept well for the first time in months.

A week later, I looked over my letter. Two things struck me forcibly: one, I realized I felt guilty for the marriage breakup, but was putting all the blame on David, my ex, and, two, I wasn't such a bad person after all. I began to put the whole experience into perspective. I acknowledged my part in allowing the marriage to become boring and David to slip into another woman's arms. I also reminded myself that I am human and not divine.

The more I considered the overall situation the more I felt understanding and not resentment toward David. I also felt more accepting of myself. This in turn reinforced my growing self-confidence.

Time eventually cemented my self-forgiveness and acknowledgment of my mixed feelings. I burned the letter somewhat melodramatically in a private, candle-lit ceremony, some six months later, when I was able to laugh at my own shortcomings. I am no longer a slave to emotional memories.

Letting the past control the present is a danger all of us face. Each single parent will have a unique set of emotional claws trying to drag him or her backward. There is no one formula for escape except these hints that the solution, as with the unease, lies within.

EX
EXERCISE

Free yourself from useless anger at your ex. There are two parts to this exercise: writing and fantasizing. First complete the list on the Ex Chart that begins, "What makes me angry at my ex." When you've finished the list, write beside each item as full an explanation as you can about why that particular trait or action irritates you. Then—and allow plenty of time for this—think about the items,

EX
CHART

WHAT MAKES ME ANGRY AT MY EX:	WHY

one at a time, and answer honestly, "Is this a fault of mine, too?"

The second part is much harder. Take five minutes a day to imagine your ex being happy. Accept this picture and sincerely wish your ex happiness, *without you.*

Screen your "happy ex" private movie in your imagination regularly for as long as necessary. Avoid drifting off into reveries of pleasurable times involving both you and your ex. The benefits of this exercise will soon be apparent: you'll feel generous and you'll be more comfortable talking with your ex.

BEFRIEND YOUR EX

Just because you don't want to live with your ex doesn't mean you can't be friends. Real friendship can develop when you have worked through the shock and sorrow of separation. For some, this takes six months, others require a couple of years or a decade. You may never reach the Olympian heights of a divorcée who insists that her ex "is my best friend. I love him. And I love his new wife, too." But you can very likely achieve the warm glow that Deborah felt when her fourteen-year-old son told her: "I'm so proud of the way you and dad have become friends and the way you help each other."

Sometimes being friendly leads to sex with the ex. This can be "for old times' sake" or because it's comforting to sleep with someone familiar. This need fades as you grow independently from your ex. In the meantime, it is important not to confuse your child who may well be fantasizing a permanent reunion.

To achieve a true friendship with your ex is to know you have triumphed over pain and perplexity. You've come to terms with your hate, anger, jealousy and disappointment. You've accepted your part of the blame for the death of the relationship. You've matured. And the bonus is your child's delight at the fracture of friction.

DIRECT YOUR ANGER PROPERLY

Anger is a familiar feeling to many single parents. Frustrated at the lack of adequate day care, irritated by inflexible employers, annoyed at their exes, anxious at the shortage of cash and furious at unfairness, single fathers and mothers react angrily. Unfortunately, some of us turn that anger onto ourselves . . . or our children.

A single parent is the chief source and measuring stick of emotions for the child, and so is under particular obligation to direct anger at the enemy. To direct the anger at the proper targets would be healthy, and right. Blow your top with the person or institution that upset you; don't take it out on your child.

On the other hand, if you *are* angry with the child, then let her know. Few things are more harmful to a child's perception of reality than the ever-calm parent. You are angry, fine. Let it out. And explain to your child why, as much as you understand yourself.

Love does not mean that you always feel kind and contented with your child. Rita, a divorcée with a young boy and girl, speak, for most single parents when she says:

I guess it's been hard at times. I've often felt tired and irritable and wanted only quiet, and then come home to two children bickering, two cats eating plants; books, shoes, socks over the floor; supper to get ready and two loads of wash that just had to get done. There never seemed to be the time for the luxury of reading without interruption. Sometimes I'd be so depressed I'd want to cry. Sometimes I did.

Now I feel I'm allowed to feel that way and can talk to the kids about it. I'm allowed to feel bitchy and just say it. "Yes, kids, I'm bitchy; I'm sorry I'm taking it out on you; but I guess you take it out on me sometimes—that's what love is all about!"

This is not to advocate hitting your child in anger. You should have sufficient control of yourself to avoid that. Punch a pillow, not a child. If you suffer uncontrollable outbursts that result in beating your child, get help fast. The crisis lines listed in the front of the telephone directory will tell you where. Or call Parents Anonymous (see Resources, page 157).

ANGER
EXERCISE

Take a look at how you handle anger. Complete the Anger Chart on pages 24 and 25.

ANGER
CHART

LAST TIME I GOT ANGRY:	WHAT I DID:

NEXT TIME I GET ANGRY I'LL . . .

ANGER
CHART

WHAT I SHOULD HAVE DONE:

SET
YOUR OWN VALUE

Set your own value, and set it high. If you have to pretend at first, that's all right. Other people will treat you accordingly. If you crawl, they'll step on you. If you march with your head held high, they'll respect you. Never put yourself down. Listen to what you say about yourself during the next five days. Every time you say something negative about yourself, you become that much more unlikeable. Be positive. Speak only of your strengths. Others will see you favorably, and you'll feel great.

One obstacle can be friends or relatives who cling to old-fashioned concepts. They may try to make you behave in the way *they* think you should. They may be eager for you to marry, for example. Avoid the trap of doing what others think you should. Being yourself is worth far more to you and your child than conforming to what you think others expect.

Avoid negative, destructive people. Your surroundings and your friends should uplift you.

"Sometimes the 'help' people give hurts your dignity," says a single mother of an eleven-year-old daughter. Often 'help' is in the form of unwarranted advice. Think for yourself and be guided by what you feel is right. Remember that no matter what someone is talking about, he is usually talking about himself. Thus the wife who counsels a single mother to "find a man" is actually talking about her own satisfaction, or, conversely, her fears, as a wife.

Don't ask, "What does this person think of me?" but, "What do *I* think of this person?"

LEARN
TO TRUST YOURSELF

Listen to your inner self. Your instincts are not infallible, but they are a good guide. If you feel uneasy or disturbed about something, don't do it. Once you have arrived at a decision, act confidently.

However, trusting to instinct or common sense alone is not enough — use your head, too. Much of what we consider natural or obvious is actually the result of our own upbringing and of current social mores. Learn useful things by reading how-to-parent books, attending classes or discussion groups. Evaluate such activities. Don't accept something as gospel because it comes from a supposed "expert." Weigh the advice. Think about the expert's vested interests. (For example, does the author/speaker have a professional stake in believing you can succeed only through long-term therapy?) Consider the uniqueness as well as the similarities of your personal family style to those being suggested.

DEVELOP
A SENSE OF HUMOR

Few people admit to not having a sense of humor. It's easy to laugh at others; laughing at yourself is quite different. Yet to be able to see the ludicrousness of your own behavior, to be amused at the incongruity of what you do can be a help. For a single parent, the test is whether you can laugh or at least smile at your own troubles and foibles:

When you loosen up, learn to laugh and can even be foolish or goofy with your kids, the relationship is more honest and open. If your children know you like them, and you can have fun together, you enjoy being a parent.

Developing this sense of humor requires sharpening our senses of observation, and listening to our children. One single mother overheard her child ask another, "Do you have a live-in or a live-out father?" Then there was the little boy who wrote in a school essay, "I have one brother, two stepfathers, a father and one mother."

We had just finished supper, "Hey, dad, that was a great meal you cooked," said my daughter. "Well, thanks," I said beaming. "I think that's the first time since you could talk that you've said something I cooked was good." She looked at me thoughtfully and said, "No, it isn't. I remember one time about three years ago. It was spaghetti, then, too."

A guide to discovering and developing your sense of humor (including LST—Laughter Self Therapy) is available in *The Laughter Book* (see Suggestions for Further Reading, page 162).

HELP
OTHERS

Helping others can be one way to uplift yourself. There are many volunteer groups that would welcome you—Red Cross or St. John

Ambulance, the cancer societies, Pro-Life, save-the-environment associations, boys' and girls' clubs—but you can also do things on your own. One of the most rewarding is described by a British single father now living in Boston:

Most of my free time is taken up with my son and, anyway, I'm not keen on joining organizations. But I remembered my old Boy Scout motto, something about doing a good deed every day, and I decided to try it.

What a difference it made to me. Deliberately trying to think of something nice to do for someone every day made me a much more cheery person. I began by paying compliments to people, doing someone a surprise favor and so on. Then I hit upon a really effective good deed. When a clerk or bus driver or someone was really doing a good job, I would send a letter to their boss, or to the newspaper, mentioning the person's name. This is even more fun than complimenting someone directly.

Mind you, it has its drawbacks. I've lost two great people at my bank— after my letter to their head office, they were both transferred and promoted!

Perhaps you'd prefer to become immersed in something all-absorbing—a cause. It has to be something you really care deeply about. Some single parents have found new meaning in their lives—and thus had more vitality to offer their children—by joining in a struggle: the struggles for adequate day care, against experiments on animals or for world government are a few examples. Maybe what impassions you is not an organized cause. Why don't you be the person who revs up the steamroller?

REWARD
YOURSELF

Just as rewarding a child for "good" behavior is more effective than punishing him for "bad," rewarding yourself for your accomplishments is much better than berating yourself for your shortcomings. Smiling at yourself in the mirror may sound ridiculous, but it is an example of one of the little things you can do to feel good about yourself. And the benefits are great, as Rita, a single mother of a twelve-year-old daughter and a nine-year-old son, found out:

I've found Rita. I've found my weaknesses and strengths—a lot of strengths. I can do whatever is necessary and still have time for me and, better yet, others.

And a twenty-one-year-old never-married mother of a delightful chubby baby discovered:

I've found that I'm stronger than I thought I would be. I didn't really think that I could manage as well as I do.

SELF-DISCOVERY
EXERCISE

Shrink your fears by building on your good points. Here's how to rediscover your strengths: on the Self-discovery Chart, list all your positive points on the left and all your negative ones on the right. Be thorough—include everything you can think of. Most of us are only too well aware of our shortcomings, so you probably won't need help for that list. But don't sell yourself short on the positive side. Write anything you're proud of, anything you remember with pleasure: relationships, skills, interests, characteristics, insights, health. Add to the chart over the next few days. If you don't mind showing the chart to a trusted friend or relative, you might discover even more positive aspects of your personality from their observations.

The next step is to review your Plus list. This reminds you of your admirable qualities and your accomplishments. You can build on these.

Now look at the Minus side. Which items have you exaggerated? Which negatives can you change? Determine now how you will wipe out those negatives one by one. Plan an attack on each item. Begin with the one you consider easiest to change, and allow yourself sufficient time to improve—this might be a matter of days or months.

Every six months, write down your current accomplishments. You'll be amazed how the Minus list shrivels and the Plus list grows.

HELP
FROM COUNSELORS

A counselor may well help a single parent overcome certain personal problems. But if it's help on practical matters you seek—finding somewhere to live, how to qualify for financial assistance, how to budget—don't get drawn into personal therapy. Many single parents have mixed emotions as they settle into the unaccustomed

SELF-DISCOVERY
CHART

PLUS	MINUS

role. It's normal. So be wary of thinking you are sick and need a professional to cure you.

Beware, too, of being put on drugs. Single parents, and especially their children, too often fall into this trap.

Your fears may be fed by faults in society at large. It's not because there's something wrong with you that there are too few day-care facilities or that housing is so expensive. But your anxiety about proper care and shelter for your child is real. The solution is not to be counseled out of your anger at such injustices but to take action to try to correct these wrongs.

If, when you are in distress, you have a friend who is able to hold you, figuratively and actually; who will accept and not lecture, then you are fortunate and will be unlikely to need a professional friend. But natural friends are often too close or otherwise ill equipped to assist you in tackling your anxieties or fears objectively. You may need someone who is accepting, friendly but detached and skilled enough to help you help yourself.

If you find yourself too down too long, you owe it to your child, let alone yourself, to get professional help. How do you find a suitable counselor? Since social workers and psychiatrists are not immune to society's prejudices, they might be blind to or accept such things as the double standard toward women, inadequate day-care and discrimination against single parents. The best way to find a good counselor is on the recommendation of someone you trust. Failing that, phone your nearest information and referral agency, hospital, crisis line, radio station, university or newspaper. City dwellers have the advantage over single parents in the country because counseling is more frequently available in urban centers.

When you meet a counselor, trust your emotional reaction to him or her. If you feel uncomfortable with this person (apart from the possibility of feeling some discomfort in discussing your problems with anyone), then find another professional. In Canada, this help is free at social agencies or through medicare. In both Canada and the United States, fee-charging counselors are available. They are listed in the Yellow Pages under Social Workers, Psychologists, Marriage and Family Counselors, etc. Psychiatrists are usually listed under Physicians and Surgeons.

A warm, trustworthy, trained listener can be very useful in aiding you to figure out your own problems. It is the relationship, and only partly the counselor's training or theories, that counts.

Your responsibility is to be as frank as possible—first with yourself and then with the professional.

Lucrezia is a Catholic single mother who searched a long time for the right professional. She was finally helped by an able counselor in a Jewish agency:

I've had the experience of a lot of contradictory advice from experts. You have to pinpoint who you're going to place your trust in. I find friends play expert a lot. You've got to stay away from listening to friends or seeking their advice.

The same thing goes with a lot of social workers, or psychologists or people at the women's center who say, "do this, do that." Well, you can get yourself into a lot of hot water. Experts don't know the whole picture. They can only see one side of it.

We all have an inner resource that we have to give ourselves time to draw on, to learn about. Running helter-skelter doesn't do anything but drain energy. Something like the Jewish Family Services I can't recommend more highly —seeing *one* person who can refer you to people he has confidence in.

You have to trust your instincts.

HELP
THROUGH FAITH

Some single parents find tremendous support in their local church groups. In many cases, these are small congregations.

Spectacular help through spiritual faith is reported by some single parents, like this one from a single mother of nine:

In my personal experience, I would have been shattered emotionally if I had not reached out for spiritual help and had many prayers answered. My help came from God, not a church building, nor a group, but in a very real and personal way. I am not overly pious, but I do know where my help came from. I have received and witnessed several miracles in answer to prayer. Many times I was literally all alone and desperate (and once facing death) and I was helped, healed and made happy.

I tell you this in all sincerity because I know that on my own I could not have made it through all the frustrations, worries and illnesses of my nine children.

THREE

OVERCOME LONELINESS

A SINGLE PARENT NEEDS CONTACT with other adults. This is especially true for those at home most of the day, but it also applies to single parents who work outside the home and who may have only superficial relationships with workmates. The need for contact with another adult affects a single parent most acutely at night, after his or her child is in bed. A single father of four confessed:

I'd sit alone at night and the cold realization would come over me that I was really on my own. I had to do it all, alone. Yes, I was very lonely.

Anne-Marie, a widow with a twelve-year-old girl, agreed that, "It's a lonely existence as far as child-rearing is concerned. But," she adds, "the rewards are great. I have a deeper bond with my daughter because I'm a single parent."

One single mother has an apt question for divorced single parents:

Were you any less lonely when you were married? I remember crying myself to sleep many nights when I was married and so-called "together."

DENIAL OR DECISION

The choice is between retreating further and further into loneliness, or determining to do something about it. The desire for companionship, for understanding and acceptance—for friendship—is normal. Denying this, you as a single parent will become increasingly bitter, shortchanging your child as well as yourself.

You may feel lonely simply being in a home that you once shared with your ex. Perhaps, like many single parents, you feel especially lonely when something—such as a couple walking hand-in-hand, the car not starting or having to prepare your own breakfast—triggers your feeling of emptiness. Don't panic. You can learn to develop rich relationships. But take your time. Your aim is to help your child by helping yourself. Avoid plunging too quickly into new alliances. Better to live a while with some loneliness than cause yourself more heartache by rushing into additional grief.

First, you must be clear about what you want. Perhaps you are like Sybil, who used to wake up during the night nervous, afraid and desperately lonely. Her first plan of action was to put new locks on the doors and windows. Sybil was wise enough to realize that casual bedmates would not resolve her acute feelings of loneliness. She decided that what she needed was contact with someone who felt as she did, someone she could trust to understand and to listen. Sybil posed this problem at a single-parent discussion group and she found such a person—Enrico. There was nothing romantic about their relationship, but Enrico agreed that Sybil could call him at any hour of the day or night. This soon meant she could sleep nights, confident in the knowledge that someone cared and that, if she did awaken, she could talk her fears out with her new friend.

In trying to alleviate loneliness, a single parent may well make the same mistake as Margaret, a thirty-year-old single mother of two: she talked endlessly with women friends in the same situation as herself. "But I found this exchanging of tales of misery only accentuated my loneliness." As another divorcée found out:

Constantly talking about your divorce and the problems you're getting from your ex makes you bitter and makes you not a nice person to know. You're going to lose friends fast.

It is good to have friends that you meet other than through your child. You will not necessarily get along with another adult just because your children are friends.

Many single parents use the telephone extensively—particularly when the child is asleep—to keep in touch with friends. This can work well until the child is old enough to stay up as late as you. In the words of a single woman who has been on her own with two children for six years:

I spend lots of time on the phone to cut loneliness. Part of loneliness is needing someone to unburden to. The phone is good for this, especially in the evenings when time is clear.

Other single parents write letters or use CB radio. Receiving letters confirms that someone cares. When you write you not only connect with the other person, you reveal yourself to *you*. Pen pals can be found through organizations such as Single Booklovers (see Resources, page 159), the classified section in newspapers or by writing a letter to the editor of a newspaper here or abroad. One widower who did this received two hundred replies.

Write your letters or chat on the phone when your child is absent or asleep. Children of single parents complain that their parents spend too much time on the phone: that's time taken away from them. Ten-year-old Jeremy suggests that, if you really can't plan your telephone talking for when the child is not around, "then set time limits in the evening—and stick to them."

For most single parents, being with other adults is preferable to talking on the phone or writing. The surest way to cut loneliness is to get out and meet people. Pleading lack of time, money or sitters is not good enough. A single woman who adopted four preteens says:

I don't understand widowed and divorced people saying, "Now that I'm single, I can't meet people." I find that the children have not handicapped me at all in meeting people. It's true that I can't go out the same as I used to, but I still seem to make a lot of contacts. It's true that there is less money for sitters, but I usually can manage it. I make an arrangement with neighbors or I save up for that occasion. Sometimes people can be kind and sit for a bit less than they would usually charge for four children.

Not every single parent is a sociable person. But all of us have some undeveloped interest—be it deep-sea diving, photography, writing poetry, karate, acting or politics—and the solution to lack of companions is to jump into activities of your choice. The activity itself should be a very real objective for you, otherwise the whole exercise will be sadly self-defeating. If you are sincerely interested in the activity, it is more likely that you will get along with other people involved in it.

Occasionally, a single parent will claim, "I'm too busy to be lonely." For some that's true, but a busy single parent may be masking, or avoiding, loneliness. Reducing loneliness is a matter of quality, not quantity. It is not keeping busy, but human interaction that nullifies loneliness. And this interaction with other adults can benefit your child, too. A truly busy single parent writes:

We have all kinds of people coming through our house. Some live here for a while. Some are frequent, others infrequent, visitors. I really relish being able to choose for myself who to invite. And there's a great benefit to the children, too. They get to meet a wide variety of people. They learn from these friends and they hear about various lifestyles and jobs and opinions they might not otherwise have a chance to appreciate. It helps them to sort out their own values.

LONELINESS
EXERCISE

Here's how you can tackle your loneliness. In one column of the Loneliness Chart, write down the times you feel lonely. For instance one of these might be just after the child is in bed. Or it may be on Sunday afternoons when you remember the things you used to do with your ex. Whatever the occasion, make a list. Consider, one by one, how to defuse them with practical actions, such as scheduling volunteer activity for Sunday afternoons. Write your intended actions in the second column. Set time limits for resolving each occasion, one by one, over the next few weeks or months.

SAVORING
SOLITUDE

You don't have to be lonely simply because you are by yourself. Each human being is ultimately alone. Positive solitude is accepting that fact and learning to enjoy times when you are physically and psychically by yourself. In essence, enjoying solitude means having a mind well stocked with fascinating material. Self-discovery can be an exciting journey.

There are many things, such as reading, painting and writing, that are often best enjoyed in solitude. But it is not a matter of filling solitude with tasks. Rather it is a finding and developing of oneself that *is* the task. (Some would add that there is a spiritual dimension: in solitude one can communicate with the Infinite.) Being comfortable by oneself is a wonderful asset. Each mind is unique—a rich, private world unto itself. The single parent, who is often alone, would do well to cultivate solitude.

LONELINESS
CHART

WHEN I FEEL LONELY:	WHAT I'M GOING TO DO ABOUT IT:

EXTEND
YOUR FAMILY

Some lonely single parents go to live with *their* parents. This rarely works out well. While it is fine for your child to be acquainted with grandparents (on your ex's side, too), the pressures of crowding and different life-styles can be too much for older parents who thought they were through raising you years ago. There is a strong likelihood that you will lean too heavily on your parents, once again picking up the role of child, at the very time that you should, for the sake of your child and yourself, be handling your life as an adult.

This is not to say, of course, that you should be isolated from your parents. On the contrary, they, and your former in-laws, can be a valuable emotional support to you and your child. They usually are extremely concerned both for you and their grandchild. Give them a chance to show this love. Send your child to them for a week or two, visit for a day or an evening, but don't, like this single father, move in on a semipermanent basis:

I regressed back to early childhood; I even wet the bed at night. It was five months before I once again began behaving like an adult.

Instead of imposing on your relatives, you might reduce loneliness by creating your own extended family or cooperative living arrangement. A single father and his children in a small town have "adopted" an old couple as "grandparents." Such a family does not have to live together, but one single mother hopes to have an extended family-by-choice on a communally owned farm. Lucille is one of several single parents who've developed an extended family-by-choice:

Children need a wider group than just the single-parent family for sharing skills and interests. We've been very fortunate with the people in our Meeting [local Quaker group]. There's always someone from the Meeting to talk things over with, most noticeably when I was first separated. The kids have a real extended family with certain people from the Meeting — they go to each other's homes, have potluck suppers, work camps. We celebrate holidays, such as Christmas, together. We do all the things families do, only we've chosen each other. We include people of various ages. It's good to know they're there.

LIVE
COOPERATIVELY

Nadine, who has a four-year-old daughter, is an enthusiastic sup-
porter of cooperative living:

I believe in cooperatives. First of all, they allow the children to come up
against other parents and the parents to come up against other children
and parents. They allow a much greater sense of freedom and a much
easier sense of responsibility. I prefer to live either alone or with more than
two people. I prefer to live with men and women. I don't like the idea of
four or five single mothers' getting together in a cooperative with their
kids. It's too female-oriented; you've got to have the male balance.

Cooperatives for single parents have other advantages. If you're on
your own as a single parent, it's too easy to become very resentful and
bitter, depending on your situation. If you've a lot of money, that's different, but most single parents are below the poverty line. And you may take
those situations out on your kids.

If you live with other people, immediately your financial situation is
cut; your worries aren't as great because economically you're sharing expenses. Plus the fact that no longer do you have to hire baby-sitters in
order to go out. It's an information-feedback network; you find out more
information living with other people. You're no longer alone; you're no
longer alienated. It's a very positive thing.

Before you rush off to imitate Nadine, carefully weigh all the pros
and cons of cooperative living for you and your children. You
don't, for example, want to be shocked like the ultra-clean single
parent who was horrified to discover, after moving in, that the
other single mother rarely washed her underwear. Nor would you
want to be victimized like one parent who was always left with the
dirty dishes.

Warning bells should ring if your tastes in food, politics, religion,
discipline or home entertainment differ radically from your prospective home-sharing family's. The exercise of drawing up a contract might help more than the contract itself. If each family
pinpoints the things important to it, agreement on the major issues
can be hammered out before setting up house together. Some potentially explosive areas you might want to clarify:

DATING

• Are dates brought back to the house?

- Are other parent(s) expected to baby-sit?
- Are sleep-over dates acceptable?

DISCIPLINE

- How much say do the children have in running the home?
- Can one parent punish children of the other(s)?
- Will children of similar age have the same bedtime?
- Will there be a written list of rules?
- How will the use of television and telephone be settled?

HOUSEKEEPING

- Will chores such as washing, shopping or cooking be shared on a scheduled basis?
- What if one parent (or child) doesn't do his or her part?
- Will pets be welcomed?
- Will children be required to help around the house?

FINANCES

- How will the rent or mortgage, utility bills, food shopping be handled?
- If the house is purchased, what will happen if one person wants to sell?
- Will the children receive allowances?
- Whose furniture will be used?

For teen-agers, the additional adjustments required in cooperative living may be too much to bear if the move coincides with separation from a parent.

JOIN A SINGLE-PARENT ORGANIZATION

Several organizations exist uniquely for single parents. Whether an organization is for you will depend on a number of factors. Also, for intangible reasons, one chapter may be better suited to you than another:

I tried and it was awful. I went to a few dances. They seemed to me to be a bunch of sad misfits; I couldn't tune in with them at all. I would get really depressed after I made abortive attempts to socialize. I went to a wine-and-cheese party at somebody's house and I went into the bathroom and I was almost in tears. I wanted to leave but I didn't know what to do. I just knew this was no way for me to rebuild my life. It wasn't offering any support or anything positive at all. I couldn't relate to the people in any way whatsoever. I felt too much like a woman on the make; none of the men seemed at all interesting to me and I just felt totally out of place. The whole scene seemed irrelevant to me.

The major organization in Canada and the United States is Parents Without Partners (PWP). This has been an invaluable support to thousands of separated, divorced and widowed parents. Alice, a divorcée with two preteen sons, is an enthusiastic member of PWP:

PWP is a nonprofit, nonsectarian, international organization for the benefit of single parents and their children. We emphasize children's programming and also adult programs to produce a healthy parent, therefore producing a healthy child. We have social activities for both families and adults. We have discussion groups, workshops in all of the individual chapters.

My chapter has about thirty members. We have a general meeting once a month with a speaker. We have at least one, sometimes two, discussions a month. We have classes that deal with lighter things such as cake decorating and fixing cars. Ages of the parents range from twenty-two to mid-fifties.

The children get to meet other children; they find out that they aren't the only ones that have only one parent. Quite often parents will join PWP because they see what it's done for the children.

Some people join to find a mate; and usually the ones who are just looking for a partner come for a few weeks and we never see them again. They wouldn't have been an asset to the chapter in the first place, because they're just looking for friendship at one level.

Our discussion groups are really the educational parts: you get to learn about yourself, what your problems are, how to deal with them. One of the big problems that anybody has, but particularly single parents, is, "If you have a problem, where do you go for help?" We have a professional advisory board to answer questions on every facet of rights and resources: social worker, family counsellor, doctor, priest, lawyer, budgeting expert, minister. We can approach all these people. Some of them speak to our group from time to time.

Canada also has One Parent Families Association (OPFA) and, in some places, (Ottawa, for example) unaffiliated city-wide organizations. One Parent Families Association is similar to PWP. Canadian members of PWP found the parent organization to oriented to American laws and situations and decided to establish an association geared more to Canada.

JOIN
A SMALL GROUP

Many small groups of single parents gather in churches, synagogues or social agencies. These groups differ from PWP and OPFA by concentrating on solving personal problems through practical or psychological discussion; they are usually led by a professional (cleric, social worker, psychologist).

Before joining any group, be sure it is the kind you are looking for. Otherwise, like this parent, you may be dissatisfied:

I'm not too pleased with the kind of course I attended. It was a group discussion for single parents. Two men and twelve women. Everybody told his story and everybody got to know one another. The theme running through was, basically, "I have failed. I can't make my life over again. Where am I going to meet people?" Week after week of this. It was more of a group-therapy thing—you know, you support each other.

I could not relate to that. I thought it would be more constructive. What I went for was survival techniques: ways of balancing budgets, what to do with children, how to establish extended families.

Many groups for single parents are open to both men and women. Men, in general, are more reluctant than women to seek help. Single fathers are no exception. They join PWP or OPFA, but otherwise seem rarely to seek help. Some do not need it. Others, who could benefit, are either unaware of the resources available or still believe that it is unmanly to admit the need for help. Several agencies find that, even when men do join, they will often drop out after a few sessions. But some men, like Colin, a separated father of five, receive a real boost by participating in a therapy group:

It had a fantastic impact on me. It prompted me to think about areas of my life I probably wouldn't have considered otherwise. The very first benefit was that it made me realize I wasn't alone. I met many intelligent, competent people who started off just as confused as me.

Groups exclusively for single mothers are often conducted by social or religious agencies. Such groups used to be only for never-married mothers. Today there are discussion groups for all kinds of single mothers in YWCAs, children's agencies, churches, mental-health societies and so on. These groups are problem oriented. Their aim is to help single mothers by having them share their experiences and difficulties. Women gain a sense of relief from knowing they are *not* alone and from being able to talk about their problems with other sympathetic adults.

Another source of help on practical, political and personal matters for single mothers is women's centers. The programs and activities vary, but a single mother is guaranteed a welcome.

FOUR

A TIME TO DREAM, A TIME TO DO

A SINGLE PARENT—unhampered by a marital partner—has a splendid chance to make dreams come true. Many single parents have carved out new careers or pursued other activities that had previously been only fantasies.

Single parenthood is a challenge, and part of that challenge is having to rearrange your life. Faced with the responsibility of raising a child, many a single parent has responded by daring to try a new life-style. Here are a few:

- A single father gave up city life and bought a farm.
- To have more time with her sons, a woman on the West Coast quit her executive-secretary job to live more simply on public assistance.
- Three single-parent familes, one headed by a father, moved in together.
- A shy, never-married mother signed up for flying, yoga and ceramics. She also started volunteer work on an Indian reserve.

For many, the first step toward realizing a dream is a change of address.

My husband didn't want me, my employer didn't want me, the landlord didn't want me. I was unwanted, unloved, unappreciated. I moved out. I found a place of my own. I figured if I decorated it the way I wanted to—made it my own—that that would be a positive step to a new start. It really did wonders for me.

Several other single parents discovered that the hard work of redecorating a new home was their turning point—and that the children felt this. Huguette, five-year-old daughter of Marlene, said, "Mummy's much happier now we've moved; she didn't like the old place."

However, although moving is great for you, it may be disastrous for your child—if it happens too soon. If you feel the disruption of your child's familiar surroundings would be too much for him to bear, then simply rearrange your bedroom.

Changing your address or transforming your bedroom has the power to make you feel good because it signifies a fresh beginning. You are on your way to achieving what you want.

BE SELFISH, RESPONSIBLY

The essence of good single parenthood is responsible selfishness: single parents best serve their children by putting themselves first. A paradox, but perhaps the most important one of all for single parents.

Precisely because your child is of paramount importance to you, should you be sure not to resign yourself to living in a child-dominated world. Pursuing your own interests will help you be a better, more relaxed, tolerant, happy parent. If, on the contrary, you box yourself in, you will inevitably resent the child and thus create two unhappy people.

The responsibly selfish single parent realizes that sacrificing self for a child is self-defeating. Doing everything for your child is not only demoralizing to the parent, it is also devastating to the child. The single parent who is constantly with the child, catering to every whim, denying outside contacts, adult relationships and self-development, is doomed to disappointment. The child will grow up self-centered and obnoxious.

A single parent should be responsibly selfish because the child will eventually leave home. If you live only for the child during the child-rearing years you will face a bleak future. Responsible selfishness also prepares you to face realistically the likelihood that your child will not express—or perhaps even feel—gratitude for your sacrifices.

If your child does appreciate your trials in raising him, that is a pleasant bonus. To expect it, however, could be condemning yourself to disillusion and the child to unfair guilt.

RETURNING
TO SCHOOL

Your dream may be simple or complicated. If it involves education and you can only attend school part-time, or study by correspondence, remember that five or six years from now you'll be five or six years older, either with or without the diploma. Why not give yourself the chance to broaden your mind? Some colleges have adapted their regular programs to more flexible schedules suitable for busy parents. Here are some examples:

- Toronto's Centennial College of Applied Arts and Technology offers a wide range of flexible programs leading to graduation in such areas as business administration and paralegal work.
- Trinity College in Burlington, Vermont, lets you earn a degree by attending class every other weekend.
- "Week-end College" at Chicago's Mundelein College was one of the first to design career programs for older women. They range from fifteen courses for a certificate to forty courses for a bachelor's degree.
- Triton Junior College in River Grove, Illinois, offers a preview session in which (for free) you can take vocational-interest tests, learn about the courses offered and chat with persons already enrolled. Before embarking on a three-year associate degree course with attendance required only two days a week, you could gear up with mini-courses that refresh or prime you in such areas as math, reading, writing, studying, memory and class presentations. Triton is typical of the kind of flexible programing now available at many colleges and universities. Majors include data processing, liberal arts, business management and accounting.
- Colorado College for Women in Denver offers a choice of individualized curricula for women keen on returning to the work force.
- Concordia University in Montreal has had a long tradition of.evening courses for working adults and is constantly adapting its programs.
- Goddard College in Plainfield, Vermont, was one of the earliest to give students credit for "life experience" and to trim residence requirements while tailoring studies to an individual's professional goals. Now there are some thirty other such "Universities Without Walls," including the Universities of Massachusetts and California at Berkeley, College of New Rochelle (in Westchester County, New

York), Stephens College (in Antioch), Florida International University and Loretto Heights College (in Denver).
• Extension courses: you can study for college credits via the newspaper through the University of California in San Diego, and via television in Nebraska, Iowa, Kansas and Missouri through the University of Mid-America. Similarly in Chicago (TV College) and New York (Sunrise Semester).

Colleges will offer more and more such flexible programs as the average age of the population increases and ordinary enrollment decreases. Canadian single parents can find out more about these opportunities from their local Manpower office or nearest community college. In the United States a central information office for single mothers wishing, or having, to join the work force is Displaced Homemakers (See Resources, page 152). Scholarship information is also available.

Several single mothers have embarked on studies at Montreal's Dawson College to become social workers with the object of helping other single parents. Another single mother spent several years supporting herself and daughter through typing while she studied at university to achieve her dream profession—to become a music therapist. The important thing is to decide what you want and to seize upon the possibilities. Don't give up before you start because you don't have the health, the education, the courage or the cash. First think big, *then* consider the obstacles and how they can be overcome. There is usually a way.

WORKING
OUTSIDE THE HOME

Some single mothers are bewildered when they return to the work force after an absence of years while married or on welfare. Others are exhilarated. Many single mothers begin working outside the home because of financial necessity and then find they enjoy it so much that they'd continue working even if they didn't have to. A job can be rewarding because it provides a break from your child (you love him, but twenty-four hours a day you don't need—and neither does he); contacts with other adults; a feeling of accomplishment (made real by that paycheck); and the development of new interests (sparked by your co-workers or the boss).

Single fathers as well as single mothers who work outside the house will need to consider the following:

• Make careful arrangements for your child in the event of an emergency. You will feel less guilty and anxious while you're at work and the child is at home. Equip your child, and the home telephone, with a list of persons and numbers to call if something unexpected happens. It is reassuring for the child or a sitter to know what to do in advance. The list should include such obvious things as police, fire, ambulance and paramedic numbers, but also information about the child's health (such as allergies, last tetanus shot and where medical records are kept), names and phone numbers of relatives, neighbors, godparents and your ex. Don't forget the address and telephone number *in the home*; a flustered person can easily make a mistake when giving emergency information. A written authorization for emergency medical care should be signed by you. In Canada, include a photocopy of your child's or your medicare card, and in the United States, your private insurance identification.

• Try to get a job close to home (less time on the road means more time with your child).

• If your employer agrees, you can gain peace of mind by telephoning your child. Train her to call you at work only when really necessary. (Be sure she always has the right change in case she's stranded away from home.) One single mother keeps a double diary listing both her and her son's appointments and activities. "I also walk around with a beeper connected to both my answering service and my son, so I'm reachable everywhere."

• Look for part-time work or a job with flexible hours—or share one job with someone else. According to a recent study by the United States National Council for Alternative Work Patterns, twenty-eight organizations currently encourage job-sharing.

• Consider establishing your own business. You could be as successful as each of the single parents who assessed her talents, needs and ambitions to start an owner-driver taxi service; parlay her way to ownership of a chain of jewelry shops; teach how to cook *a la chinoise*; breed rabbits; make, teach and sell ceramics; gain control of a construction company.

FIND TIME
FOR YOURSELF

A single parent has to have time free from the child to stay sane and to realize a dream. Yet many, especially those with only one small child, either think this is impossible or feel too guilty to be absent from the child to do something pleasurable for themselves.

It is true that a small child should never be left alone even while sleeping. But it is equally true that a single parent has to have a break sometimes. Your identity has to be beyond being simply "Johnny's mother" or "Susan's father."

Finding time for yourself can be hard if you are a single parent with little income and several children. Here is how one never-married mother with three children under six handles the challenge:

My whole day is for the children till eight o'clock. At 8:00 everyone's off to bed. From 8:00 to 2:00 in the morning is my time. I can do whatever I want to a certain extent—I don't make a lot of noise. I don't want to go to bed early because then my time seems less. I've trained myself to sleep from 2:00 to 7:30 A.M. I can take a bath, watch TV, talk on the phone, read. This way the day is stretched and I have time, too.

Anita, a single mother of two, say it's a matter of priorities:

If I need extra sleep, well I just take it—when everything else is done of course—except chores or crappy stuff like sorting laundry or scrubbing pots, that just doesn't have priority.

Single parents have come up with several methods of finding time for themselves. Some of these arrangements include beneficial side effects. For example, sharing living quarters with other single parents means not only being able to go out occasionally, but also cutting living costs and loneliness.

One single mother in the West found an order of nuns that provided refuge for her son while freeing her to work and play. Most fortunate is the single parent whose ex or relatives are happy to provide warm, family sitting.

Organized play groups, one or two afternoons a week, are another way single parents of preschoolers can snatch a few private hours. You may have to organize your own play group. It's not as hard as it sounds, especially after you find another parent to help. Parents can be reached through notices in churches, supermarkets, schools, YMCAs, local papers and laundromats. You can chat with parents in parks and playgrounds.

SITTERS:
MORE THAN TIME-GIVERS

Single parents should be particularly alert to the importance of sitters. They are not just sitting in your home watching your material possessions—they are responsible for your child. After parents and teachers, their job is probably third in importance. In an emergency, your child's life may depend on the sitter.

Sitters should know what you want them to do in an emergency. Whenever possible, they should have the phone number where you can be reached. They should be in sympathy with your methods of discipline and your life-style, otherwise unpleasant confusions could arise for the child.

Every sitter should be carefully screened by you, observed in action with the child, liked by the infant, have references, not be in conflict with your attitudes and be paid well.

Paying well is difficult for many single parents. If it's a problem for you, try to work out some arrangement with other single parents to alternate sitting. You might, for instance, gain two free nights or days each week by sitting once for two other single-parent families, each of whom takes a turn looking after all the children. This is especially beneficial for the children because they mix with another single-parent family. Or a teen-ager from another single-parent family might sit with your child in return for some skill or service you can offer (e.g., teaching a language, sewing clothes, chaperoning a party, repairing a bicycle).

Single fathers sometimes have difficulty hiring a teen-age girl sitter. Why not employ a boy? Why should only girls be sitters? If there are no boy sitters in your area, or for some reason you prefer to leave your child with a girl, here's how other single fathers have solved the dilemma of suspicious teen-age sitters:

• Meet the prospective sitter's parents to reassure them that you do have a baby and that you are not a dirty old man.
• Ask a previous sitter to vouch for you.

- Advertise (in local paper, supermarket, church, single-parent group) for a "father's helper." Potential sitters know right away that you are raising the child alone.
- Find a mature-woman sitter who is not nervous about single men.

You can find sitters through friends, high school counselors, newspaper ads or, better still, by "knowing people through being involved in community action groups," says Lucille, a teacher and single mother of two teens.

Or you can start a Rent-A-Mum business. This matches older women who want a sense of belonging to young families desperately in need of help. Begun by a single mother in Illinois, Rent-A-Mum does more than provide stopgap baby-sitting. The substitute mothers receive an hourly wage, the organizer gains a little financial profit, the child is in experienced hands, the single parent has peace of mind and perhaps picks up child-raising or cooking hints.

Every single parent who works outside the home and has a child in elementary school has to cope with the problem of the school day's being shorter than the work day, not to mention school holidays, snowstorms and strikes that shut schools or terminate transportation. It is best to make lasting arrangements with sitters, neighbors and relatives as soon as possible and not leave them to the last minute.

A child should be taught how to use the telephone for emergencies. Be sure the child is always equipped with change. There must be a neighboring home, church or even a store where your child could wait for a few minutes if you are unexpectedly delayed getting home. Make such preparations in advance, so your child is not left sobbing and frightened on the street. Perhaps you could start a "block parent" group. Check with your local police or school.

An excellent after-school location is the local library. There your child could do homework in safe surroundings. Or you might take turns with other families in your neighborhood in providing an afternoon snack for several children. If your work schedule prohibits you from taking a turn any weekday afternoon, suggest something else you might do for the other parents (for example, having all the children at your home on a Saturday morning, or taking them on a short outing Sunday afternoons). Encourage your local Y or school board to start an after-school program or begin a drive for your community to have its own Boys' and Girls' Club. Such clubs are set up expressly to provide a broad range of children's activities.

Some single parents string a key around the child's neck, allowing access to the house, even when alone. This is not to be recommended unless the child is unusually responsible. There is too much daylight crime in our cities and too many temptations and dangers in an empty house.

A few fortunate single parents are able to take their youngsters to the workplace. This has worked successfully for Ahmed, an account executive with an advertising agency. His co-workers and the boss think Ahmed's four-year-old son is adorable: he never lacks for playmates and attention. Such openness and flexibility by employers and other employees is rare and perhaps more acceptable in creative environments. Single mothers working in a treatment center for disturbed children were encouraged to bring their infants and, said a staff psychologist, the result was not a loss in efficiency "but, rather, an increase in motivation."

RELAX, REFRESH, RECREATE

People relax in different ways. For your own mental health and happiness of your child, you should make time to have fun in the way that pleases you. Very likely there are time and financial limitations. Think imaginatively and you'll probably find a way despite the restrictions.

Some single parents find physical exertion, such as jazz ballet or tennis, excellent for releasing tension. You may refresh yourself with a simple nap, a good book, a long warm bath. Others find that listening to, or playing, music enlivens them. Some people need more risky pursuits such as sky-diving. Still others find recreation through writing.

Whatever your interests, there is a way you can indulge them even though you are a single parent. You have an obligation to yourself to do things you enjoy. They may be as simple as window shopping or as complex as studying for a law degree. Whatever the activity, whether a pastime, career, hobby, studies or sport, it will help you feel and be better. This is bound to contribute to your child's emotional growth.

DON'T SPEND TIME
BLINDLY

Time, energy and money are sometimes lost by single parents blindly doing things they think parents *should* do. Anne-Marie, an occupational therapist, made such a discovery:

I felt I had to make a hot supper every night; I rushed to have it ready for myself and my daughter when she came home from kindergarten. After a while of this pressure I realized I was being foolish—Samantha has a good lunch at school and I have a hot meal at work. We didn't need another big meal in the evening. What's more, I don't even like cooking.

You can save time by doing two things at once. No, not by cleaning the oven and checking your child's homework, but by mending clothes and watching TV, listening to the news on the radio and cooking breakfast, taking a bath and reading a magazine, putting on makeup and supervising your daughter's bath. Your teen-age children are probably adept at combining homework with listening to loud music. How many more combinations can your family come up with?

Single parents often talk to themselves. You can make further use of this useful technique for thinking things through by talking into a tape recorder while doing dishes or dusting the furniture. You could create poems, "write" notes to yourself, leave a message for the children or the sitter or just fool around singing or saying funny things that you can play back later for a good chuckle. One single mother has yet another use for a tape recorder:

I've recorded my child's favorite bedtime stories on tape. When I can't be there, or when I'm too worn out to read the same old story over again, my daughter leafs happily through her book hearing my voice telling her a story. If she wants a repeat she just has to press a button.

Some single parents use tape recorders to complement the photos they take so they have live memories of the child for later on. One single parent exchanged tapes of her children with their father, who was living in another country.

You can also use the machine to cool your temper. Pour out your anger to the recorder; it won't talk back. You'll feel better, and later, you can laugh at hearing how excited you were. One of the best uses of a tape recorder for single parents is to record yourself when you yell at the children. (Turn the machine on just before mealtime.) Listen to yourself later and you may find the reason your children speak to you the way they do: as one girl told her single mother, "That's how you speak to me." A final suggestion for the use of a tape recorder is for single-parent children to pretend to be reporters interviewing each other about their opinions of single parents. This is an excellent way to get to know the children's real feelings.

Some single parents use a timer to "give" themselves time: they can relax on the sofa for ten minutes confident in the knowledge that supper won't burn. By using the timer, they're also able to limit phone calls, oust unwanted visitors and wrap up housework.

PLAN
YOUR TIME

A single parent quickly learns that he or she must organize time and plan things in advance to get the most out of life. As Katrina, divorced three years ago, says:

Time becomes very precious, especially for a working parent or a student parent. You've got to remake a whole new social circle. But this is the time to do it. If you've always wanted to play bridge, go out and play bridge. No more excuses.

A single working woman with four children finds it necessary to be efficient:

I'm very organized. Everybody helps, starting from the beginning of the day by making their own beds. I do breakfast during the week and the children do breakfast on the weekends. Lunches we've all prepared the night before. In the afternoon, one of the children will help me in the kitchen. They have specific jobs such as stacking dishes, and one will make porridge for the next day.

Jessica, who has two preteens, points out that it is a question of priorities:

I leave for work around 7:30 a.m. Beds made—breakfast given—dishes washed—kids dressed. My daughter makes sure her scatter-brained brother doesn't forget his lunch or books or teeth brushing and the kids leave about 8:10. They come home at 4:30—snack, relax (or fight) and I'm home at 5-5:30. All doctors' and dentists' appointments are made on my half-day off. Cooking, laundry, tidying is done in the evenings and on weekends. The children help.

There's always time to help with homework, to play a game of Scrabble or cards or start a craft project. Certain things take priority. A long walk on a balmy evening after supper is more important than dusting furniture. Of course, I made the compromise of taking a lower paying job, but one that has good hours and free weekends.

TIME MANAGEMENT
EXERCISE

Here's how you can rearrange your time to make the most of each day. In an exercise book, mark off sufficient time slots to carry you through the day, by each hour or blocks of two or three hours. Prepare enough pages to cover three weeks. Then fill in your activities, hour by hour, day by day. If your child is old enough, let him join in the fun of recording where your time is going.

At the end of the three weeks examine your time log closely. See where most of your time is going by totting up the totals. How much is being spent on constructive actions? How much in routine tasks? How much is being lost and how much is being invested in your child? Select the hours you want for yourself.

List how much time you are spending each week on each of your activities and enter the totals on the Time Management Chart. Put them in order from most time spent at the top, to least at the bottom. Are these your priorities? Is this how you want to pass the coming year?

If not, list your activities in order of your real preferences. Then reallocate available time. Maybe, for example, you can lop off ten hours from passively watching television and substitute five hours of playing with your child and five hours of studying something new.

TIME MANAGEMENT
CHART

ACTIVITY	TIME SPENT			TOTAL
	WEEK 1	WEEK 2	WEEK 3	
Time with child _____				
Cooking _____				
Watching television _____				
Eating _____				
Cleaning house _____				
Exercising _____				
Sleeping _____				
Work (outside the home) _____				
Traveling _____				
Reading for relaxation _____				
Daydreaming _____				
Personal (washing, etc.) _____				
Telephone chatting _____				
Visiting _____				
Washing, ironing _____				
Sex _____				
Studying _____				
Hobbies _____				
Others _____				

FIVE

CUT EXPENSES
EAT WELL AND
CONTROL CHORES

TIME IS NOT THE ONLY THING that a single parent finds essential to budget. Money is another. Katrina has had to make drastic adjustments from her wealthy predivorce lifestyle:

When you're feeding yourself and three children on $25 a week compared to $150 you've really got to study and learn and develop survival techniques as to how to beat the supermarket.

You have to boil down to your basic five areas of nutrition and get the most for your money. I type the week's menus in advance, derive the shopping list from that. I take only the money necessary. (I used to charge and have everything delivered.) No extras. No cookies or cakes or anything that is not nutritional. We learned to make our own yogurt, etc. Meat is the biggest thing to cut down on.

Single fathers often report that family expenses go up when the wife has gone. One cause is unfamiliarity with buying or mending children's clothes. Another is the self-defeating practice of trying to buy the child's affection—or perhaps assuage guilt feelings—by purchasing goodies. This practice stops as soon as the single father feels less anxious.

Controlling expenditures proved to be a satisfying part of the new independence of one single mother:

I am in charge of my own money, which I really like. I like not having to share the responsibility of handling the budget. This surprises me because all the time I was married I kept wishing I had a husband who could handle money well and could pay the bills and I wouldn't have to worry about the bank account.

Now that I'm managing my own money, I always have enough in the bank and I've worked out my retirement. Even with inflation and strikes and everything else I seem to be able to stay ahead.

CONSERVE
YOUR CASH

You, too, can stay ahead if you apply the same principles to money as you do to time. Involve your child for added benefit: you'll be deciding on goals as a family, so your child will better understand the financial facts. Limits on spending will be clear and you won't need to nag, "We can't afford it." Start while the child is very young. Leila is seven years old and her never-married mother, Pamela, thinks friends find her more mature than seven-year-olds from coupled families,

probably because I talk with my daughter about the realities of everyday life: what money we have left out of my salary to pay bills, the importance of saving, what we can and cannot buy at the grocery store.

Budget guides are available free from banks (you don't have to have an account to ask questions or lift a leaflet), credit unions and social agencies. Here are some general guidelines:

- What are your financial desires? (Do you want a car, vacation, stereo, farmhouse, better furniture, funds for your child's education or your retirement?) Whatever your goals, make two lists: one short-term and one long-term. Arrange each list from highest priority to lowest. Mark each item L for luxury or N for necessity.
- What is your income? If your total revenue comes from welfare and, in Canada, family-allowance checks, you know the exact amount. But some single parents have income from their ex, jobs, boarders, investments or relatives.
- Keep track of your expenditures for two months.
- Compare your outgo for those two months with your income. Is this where you want your money to go? Can your priorities be met? Are all your N items *really* necessities? (For example, could transportation expenses be cut by switching from a car to a bicycle?)
- Always pay yourself first. Take off the top of your income whatever amount you have decided to save.

• If you're drowning in debts, check whether there's a Credit Counseling Service nearby. In some cities, government, business and
unions together provide this service free for persons who need help
to sort out their floundering financial affairs.

Feeding several children and an adult on one salary can be difficult:

The food bill is horrendous, but I've been consistently changing our eating
pattern. I've looked very carefully to see what the basic requirements are. I
find we eat more cheaply if I'm careful. We can't always shop at the cheapest store because when you're working you don't have time to run around
three different stores to see who has the best specials that week. I know the
stores around here, though. I may shop once a month in a different store
for a big order if I know there are a lot of things there that would be helpful. I always buy the cheaper thing. For example, we always use powdered
skim milk. It wasn't any question of whether we liked it, we had it. There
were a few complaints the first week but I said, "Tough. Do you want to
have money to go to the amusement park in the summer or don't you?"
Well, of course they did. We don't eat very much meat, certainly by the
standards to which I was brought up, so I have to compensate with eggs,
cheese and beans. It seems to be working out well because everyone seems
healthy. Fruit is not as easy to have every day as it was, but I make sure
they have it three or four times a week. Likewise with salads. They have a
raw carrot or salad at least three times a week. I always buy bread when
it's on sale. I buy thirteen or fourteen loaves, as many as I can stack in the
freezer. We use a lot of minced meat because you can do it a thousand different ways. Also I'll have eggs one night a week and fish one night a
week.

Another single mother describes how she reduces expenses:

One of our economies is that we don't have a car. That cuts down on what
you pay but it is certainly inconvenient at times. For shopping—well,
we're near shops. If I have to order I do, but delivery is expensive so I try
not to order more than once a month. Other times we go on a pilgrimage:
each of us walks down the road with a huge parcel. This may not be so
easy when they're teen-agers and wouldn't be seen dead with me and par-
cels, but we'll worry about that when the time comes.

Few single parents are wealthy. Here's how some keep expenses
down. (Many of these tips are from a woman who has been raising
her nine children alone since 1970.)

FOOD

- Shop on a full stomach (you'll be less tempted to buy unnecessary extras).
- Exercise iron control or shop without your children.
- Take only the amount of cash you can afford to spend.
- Buy individual packages of goat's milk cheese (rich but cheap).
- Use powdered milk for cooking; mix with fresh milk for drinking (2 percent is cheaper and less fattening).
- Resist television ads and buy house or no-name brands (it's often the same soup, beans or juice dressed in a different label).
- Buy hamburger in large, freezer lots, repackage in aluminum foil and freeze until needed.
- Fowl on sale can be a bargain. Buy it whole, cut up portions yourself, rewrap and freeze. You save labor costs as well as money.
- Avoid meat and eat more alternates such as baked beans, eggs, fish.
- If you are a coffee drinker, consider switching to tea. (It's about half the price per cup.)
- Buy in bulk—but only if you can really use all the product; share the purchase with other cost-conscious single parents.
- Fix a budget for food and stick to it. Adding up the cost as you shop helps to eliminate foolish purchases.
- Make a list of foods you want based on next week's or next month's menu and stick to it. Before you shop, check what's on hand in the kitchen. Make a note of items running low.
- Look for specials in newspapers, stores and your mailbox. Make sure they really are specials. Avoid impulse buying. Cash in coupons, but only for food you truly want.
- Compare the unit price of similar foods.
- Buy day-old bread and bakery goods; buy other food that's on sale if it fits into your menus. (Or adapt the menus.)
- Use stale bread in bread puddings, or rolled out with a rolling pin in breading meats, making salmon patties or stuffing.
- Make your own Popsicles by freezing fruit juices.
- Grow or at least pick your own vegetables, berries or fruit.
- Join a food co-op: you'll benefit not only from lower prices (the co-op buys in bulk and members don't have to pay a middleman) and healthier food but from meeting new people.
- Use very ripe bananas (cheap) immediately for baking.
- Potatoes are one of the cheapest yet most nutritional items you can buy—if you eat them complete with skins.

CLOTHING

- Shop in thrift stores.
- Swap clothes with other families.
- Buy from department stores only during sales; restyle or alter to fit.
- Make clothes yourself.
- Do not buy out-of-season clothes for children (they'll probably have outgrown the clothes when in season).

LAUNDRY

- Use one dependable detergent and Javex instead of several different preparations for various jobs.
- Hang your wash on a drying rack or clothesline instead of pouring money into a dryer.
- Add one cup of white vinegar to rinse cycle in place of expensive fabric softeners.

TOYS

- Make games, toys and crafts from things most people put in the garbage: plastic containers, straws, Popsicle sticks, aluminum boxes, spools, berry boxes, shoe boxes, coffee cans, plastic vinegar bottles, Javex containers.
- Use ends of wallpaper rolls for drawing and for doll houses, or ex-toilet paper rollers for "moving pictures" set up like two scrolls, using a cardboard box for the picture frame/stage.
- Make puppets out of old socks.
- Use shag remnants and other scrap material for doll furniture, drapes and rugs.
- Save old buttons for toss games.
- Slice old broom or mop handles to make checkers.
- Make modeling clay out of flour, salt, water and food coloring.

OTHER

- Take a fix-it or carpentry course (the investment pays off when you save on labor bills for home repairs or when you can adapt furniture yourself).
- Develop money-making hobbies (for example, photography, pottery, woodcarving, hairdressing).
- Cut hair at home: invest in a hair-clipping set.
- Save soap ends, soften and use in an old piece of nylon or cloth made into a mitt.

- Clean your oven with ammonia instead of costly brand-name oven cleaners. (Turn off a warmed oven, put a saucer of ammonia on the top shelf and a large pan of boiled water on the bottom. Leave overnight; wipe clean with soap and water in the morning.)
- Do your own painting and wallpapering. Share the work with friends and then do theirs. The farmers' traditional work bee was a great idea for strengthening friendships and getting the job done more easily at the same time. Involve your child for added benefits.
- Reusable plastic containers are cheaper than plastic wrap (margarine containers come with the product).
- Sew your own clothes, cushions, drapes, slipcovers, quilts, sheets. Knit socks, mitts, scarves, caps.
- Grow your own unusual indoor plants from carrot tops and seeds from grapefruit, oranges, green peppers.
- Take a homemade lunch to work.
- Use old shower curtains as effective, thicker-than-usual mattress covers for bed-wetters; also as drop cloths when painting.
- Wash windows with hot, soapy water then shine squeaky clean with newspapers.
- Make your own furniture polish: mix and shake well one-third cup each of boiled linseed oil (available in hardware stores), turpentine and white vinegar.
- Find out which kind of bank account is best for you. (For example, you may prefer the kind that provides you with monthly statements and your cancelled checks; a daily interest account is better when the balance fluctuates; in Canada, a trust company account will often be free of service charges.).
- Check inexpensive women's magazines and tabloid papers for tips on how to save money.
- Walk or bicycle instead of driving; for out-of-town trips, buses are usually cheaper, although trains are more comfortable (and usually have toilets—essential for a child).
- Buy the largest size you can of such big-use items as detergents. (But check if it is really cheaper per ounce.)
- Use credit cards *only* if you are certain you can control your expenditures *and* pay off the bills each month before interest piles up.
- Stop smoking.
- Pay utility bills in person during regular shopping trips instead of spending money on stationery and stamps.
- Ask other single parents for cost-cutting ideas: don't be shy, begin by sharing some of your own tips.

- Let clothes (and dishes) air dry instead of using machines.
- Save energy: don't heat rooms you're not using. Let the sun shine in during the day to warm the house; keep the heat in at night by drawing the drapes. Don't waste hot water by letting taps leak. Instead of draining hot bath water, open the bathroom door and allow the cooling water to warm other rooms.
- Turn off your electric stove a little before the kettle boils or food is finished cooking. The remaining heat will finish the job without waste.
- If you like to eat out, look for "Businessmen's Lunches" in Canada and "Early Bird Specials" in the United States. The same meal later is up to twice the price.
- Buy from factory outlets. These wholesale dealers sell almost everything—from clothes to carpets. They're usually listed in the Yellow Pages. If you can't find them (even under Wholesalers), in the United States ask your state's Country Agricultural Extension Service for help.
- If you're on long-term medication, you might save money by buying in bulk. Check with your pharmacist.
- Prescription drugs may be cheaper under their generic name—or at another pharmacy. Shop around.
- Buy a manual-defrost refrigerator and a stove with an oven *you* clean: cheaper to buy and cheaper to run.
- Don't pay too much income tax. Ask your tax office for up-to-date information on such things as child-care credits.

FOCUS ON
FOOD

Smart single parents become less fussy about mealtime rituals (three courses, placemats, etc.) and more concerned about nutrition. They develop shortcuts to preparing good meals swiftly. Some single parents swear by the slow cooker, an ideal way to have hot supper ready when you arrive home from work. A child can be enlisted, progressing from washing lettuce to cooking supper. Lists help, as a single father attests:

I plan menus for twelve days. That is, twelve suppers. There were seven different but nutritious breakfasts and a few suggestions for box lunches. The list of suppers saves me the bother of deciding every night what to cook. Having twelve recipes means we won't get bored with the same old food because a meal would only be repeated every second or third week. When the children visit their mother on weekends I try new gourmet recipes with girl friends or I eat leftovers in relief at not having to cook a full meal for the children.

Diet is important in strengthening happy single-parent families. Behavior problems, even some kinds of mental illness, can be linked to diet. If you are worried about your child's behavior, take a close look at what your family is eating before blaming your single status for your child's problems. Apart from allergies to specific foods (milk is a prime candidate), a child can have mild to severe reactions to the wide range of additives and preservatives in our foods . . . especially junk food.

"Junk foods are not good for anyone," says Hugh Pearson, executive director of the Society for Emotionally Disturbed Children in Montreal, "but certain children who are vulnerable can have illness triggered by an overabundance of junk food, with sugar being the main villain." And remember, junk is not *cheap*.

Single parents can easily fall into slapdash behavior for breakfast. Don't. Children will be more alert, healthier and better able to benefit from school if they have a good breakfast. Don't be restricted to traditionally accepted breakfasts. There is no reason, except inhibition, why you can't eat cold chicken, a fresh orange, a baked potato and a cup of milk first thing in the morning. What is important is that the meal be nourishing and full of protein. Look skeptically at packaged cereals.

Many single parents have to leave for work very early. If you're rushed, or even gone, at breakfast time and your child is too young to cook, you can, with some imagination, prepare a suitable, tasty breakfast the night before and have it ready in the refrigerator. Simple, nutritious recipes can be found in children's cookbooks.

Nutritional information is generally available from the United States Department of Agriculture from its national and state offices. State universities often provide similar services. Three Canadian sources are listed on pages 155 and 156.

HANDLING
HOUSEWORK

Ten years ago, most single fathers were ill prepared for the tasks and challenges of housekeeping, shopping and child raising. The women's movement has had some impact on this deplorable situation and many single fathers today handle these jobs with competence and dispatch. Like Ted: "I wash dishes and so on because these things have to be done. My children were soon enlisted in helping out." Another father who began single parenting without any housekeeping skills avoids dishwashing altogether by eating off paper plates. Washing clothes was a challenge, too:

At first I seemed to always be doing laundry. After a while I figured out that if I bought enough clothes to last me and the boys for three weeks, I'd only have to do one big wash every second Tuesday.

Single fathers may discover a new satisfaction in cooking. And, because of the conditioning of women in our society, many single fathers have little difficulty in finding women to volunteer as cooks, housecleaners or baby-sitters.

But for single parents—men and women—who are not well prepared for such chores, here are some tips from those who have learned from experience:

- Clean when you see the need. It is far easier to wipe the grease off a counter immediately than after it has become congealed.
- When a chore's a bore, nab it with habit: build the chore into a routine. This way you don't waste time thinking but not doing.
- Wiping the bathroom mirror with toilet paper when the mirror is steamed over from your shower is an example of the easy way to clean a house. Piling up housework and tackling it in a mammoth effort once or twice a month is the hard way. Basic tools, such as a vacuum cleaner, are worth the investment. Children can use them to help out. By similar reasoning, an automatic dishwasher can be a wise purchase. But the main benefit of such appliances should be the time freed to "play and be and share with the kids," as one parent puts it.
- Commercial laundries are an expensive way for a single parent to get the family's clothes cleaned. Although such laundries do an excellent job, the clothes become ragged after a while. Washing clothes at home is not hard, with a good machine. Many drip-dry clothes can be done by hand. The apartment-dwelling single parent's best bet for washing clothes is either the laundromat or a machine in a friendly neighboring high-rise. In either case, the cost is fairly low and the possibilities of making new friends high. (You

can learn a lot about a person from his or her laundry.) Incidently, ring-around-the-collar is swiftly cured with a little application of dishwashing liquid.

- Both dishes and clothes are easier to wash if they have been pre-soaked (not, though, together).
- To protect toddlers, bathroom doors should have an *outside* lock high up, and no inside lock. Anything dangerous that can be swallowed by a small child should be out of reach.
- B.S. is a versatile aid no single parent should be without. B.S. is, of course, baking soda. Quite apart from its use in cooking, baking soda has the marvellous attributes of absorbing smells (useful in your fridge and diaper pail), reducing swellings (great for that mosquito bite), removing itches (particularly good in a warm bath for little girls with minor, but very common, vaginal itch), extinguishing fires (grease and electric), cleaning (kitchen surfaces and dogs' coats), soothing burns and even deodorizing kitty litter.
- A memo board on or near the refrigerator lets you and your child note items that are running out before it's too late. Also, you can list foods and sundries that you might otherwise forget and new things someone in the family would like to try.

SIX ──────────

FIGHT PREJUDICE
AND
DISCRIMINATION

SINGLE PARENTS MEET PREJUDICE in many areas. Ten of these are: housing, employment, legal, schools, media, language, social, credit, welfare and day care.

HOUSING

Many single parents—women more so than men—encounter discrimination when searching for a place to live.

When I first had to look for a flat by myself, I was incredulous at the humiliating questions and couldn't quite cope with it. I did, finally, find a very nice place and I am truly grateful that my landlord never humiliated me.

This single mother is a level-headed, fully employed, capable person. Why should she be humiliated and "truly grateful" when she finally meets a landlord willing to rent to her?

Single mothers face double discrimination: against children and against women living alone. To some landlords, children present a specter of noise and potential damage through willful or inadvertent acts; a woman alone might be unable to pay the rent, or at the other extreme, too able because of a constant stream of male "visitors." If the single mother has a job, such a landlord may worry that unsupervised children at home may be rowdy and disturb other tenants. Similarly, a loan officer may look askance at a single mother seeking a mortgage. He (sometimes she) knows that, even if the woman is employed, her earnings will be substantially less than a man's in a similar job, and that most women employees are considered expendable and undependable. (Thus, despite evidence to the contrary, one prejudice builds upon another.)

One landlord asked a single mother who would be living in the apartment. When she answered, "My family—my son, and I," he responded, "That's not a family." This concept—that a single-parent family is "incomplete"—is pervasive and invidious. Single fathers also encounter this prejudice. Raoul, who has been separated for nine years, and his two children had a difficult time trying to rent a house:

First there were a number of landlords who flatly refused to rent to me because of the kids. That this was against the law [in Quebec] didn't bother them. They'd come up with the, "Oh, well, so-and-so who saw the place last night has decided to rent it" routine. The discrimination against kids was bad enough. What I was not prepared for was prejudice against me just because I'm single. I was amazed. Here I've been raising the kids for eight years—washing, ironing, cooking, all the things every parent does— and these loony landlords were treating me as though I didn't know how to lift a dish rag! It seems they assumed we'd be floundering in filth because there's no woman in the house. I finally found a place to rent by being less outspoken about being a single father. The landlord had just finished showing the house to me when he asked, "Wouldn't your wife like to see it before you sign the lease?" I answered, quite truthfully, "No, she wouldn't."

What can single parents, particularly single mothers, do? As with most instances of discrimination, they can try reasoning, lying or fighting.

The single parent who opts for reasoning should consider going prepared with documents that might help calm the landlord down: references from employers, testimonials from previous landlords and a cleric, a statement from the bank as to credit-worthiness and best of all, cash. If you can afford to offer the landlord several months' rent in advance, he or she will hardly consider you a potential pauper.

It is understandable that a single mother, desperate for a home for her and her children, will pretend to be married or will get a male guarantor or otherwise conform to the landlord's expectations. It's equally understandable that a single father will pretend to have a wife, or to be a bachelor. But such actions are harmful in the long run. They undermine the single parent's self-image and tarnish the reputation of single parents in general.

The single parent who decides to fight has a number of options. First, go armed with knowledge of your rights. Provincial or state laws may forbid such discrimination. If so, you can point this out and quietly explain what legal steps you have a right to take. A landlord can circumvent even the toughest laws, so be aware that these steps may have to be taken. A recent survey by the United States Department of Housing and Urban Development shows that single black women face more than a 75 per cent chance of discrimination when looking for an apartment. While United States law forbids discrimination based on race and in some areas, sex, landlords are generally quite free to refuse to rent to you because of your age, occupation or because you have children.

If the refusal to rent comes from a janitor, don't pick on him or her. Find out from municipal records or a real-estate agency who owns the building. It pays to go to the top. The president of a trust company does not relish the idea of your marching into his plush office, especially with children in tow. Even less will he like being invaded by an organized group of parents and children and newspeople. Of course, such pressure is used only after quieter methods have failed.

In any particular situation, the parent should take whatever legal recourse is available and, with friends or an organized group (such as a tenants' rights organization), apply pressure to the landlord through pickets and media publicity. In the general situation, you can, with others, gather examples of discrimination (dates, places, names) and pester the municipal, provincial or state and federal authorities to pass and implement adequate antidiscrimination laws.

Single parents can sidestep discrimination in renting (or perhaps meet mortgage prejudice head-on) by setting up formal or informal cooperatives. Some are long-term, involving the purchase of a building by its occupants. Others can be a simple sharing of rented accommodation.

EMPLOYMENT

Discrimination against single parents, particularly women, is common in employment. Single mothers, along with most women, are segregated into lower-paying jobs. It is well known that women (despite the federal Human Rights Act in Canada and the Civil Rights and Equal Pay Acts in the United States) receive less pay than men for the same work (anywhere from 40 to 80 percent less, according to the Canadian National Council of Welfare). More critical is the practice of paying women less because the kind of work they do in "female" jobs is considered of less value than the kind of work men do (for example, operating a sewing machine compared with operating a lathe). Human Rights Commissioners in Canada have found, on at least two occasions (the second involving three thousand persons), that the Canadian Federal Government has violated its own 1978 law by paying some employees (mostly women) less than it paid others for work of equal value. According to a union official, the government did not deliberately discriminate against women, but was basing salaries on those in the private sector, and, thus, "reinforcing the discrimination that exists outside of government." Even within trade unions, women face many of the same problems of discrimination that plague them in the working world. Now that women make up nearly 30 percent of union membership (compared with 15 percent in 1967), more attention is being paid to inequalities such as discrimination against women in pension plans and insurance coverage.

Inequality in the labor market hurts single mothers more than childless women because, if employers are reluctant to hire women ("You'll leave to get married," "You'll get pregnant"), they are even more hesitant to hire single mothers ("Who'll look after your kids while you're at work?" "You'll be taking time off when the kids are sick"). Although it's against the law for an employer to ask about marital status or child-care arrangements, many single mothers discover that they can't get even the most menial job without satisfying the employer's curiosity. You can report infringements of the law to your provincial or federal Human Rights Commission in Canada, or to your local or State Equal Employment Opportunity Commission in the United States.

I've never been married and I'm fed up with bosses, when they know I'm single with a child, coming on strong and trying to play the man in my life.

It's very hard to prove you've been turned down because you're a woman or because you've got kids. I filed a couple of complaints with the commission, but it took ages for a hearing and I had to get work in the meantime. So I ended up explaining my life story and how my kids are well looked after and the damn boss needn't worry that I'd be goofing off. I *need* to work. I've got three mouths to feed and a mortgage to pay off.

One of the questions I was asked for the last job was, "Did I have a boy-friend?" Now, your average teen-age girl looking for a job is not asked if she has a boyfriend. But the previously-married woman is asked.

Even other women in the work force may discriminate against single mothers. According to a recent survey, nearly 60 percent of working women believe that "A woman's place is in the home." Among those who work outside the home, a majority (mostly single, childless or older, married women) work for status, fun or investment. Single mothers, in contrast, go out to work "to feed the children." While a job provides many less tangible benefits, the salary enables a single-parent family to survive.

Action is often fast on complaints filed about abuses of mini-mum-wage laws, possibly because the issues are clearer than in hiring situations. Time sheets and pay slips can be used as evidence if a man is paid more overtime than a woman, or a woman is being paid less for work that's as responsible and demanding as work being done by a man. Such complaints should be made to pro-vincial Minimum Wage Commissions or the Wage and Hour Di-vision of the United States Department of Labor.

Beside filing for legal rights, what else can single mothers do about discrimination in the work force?

• Learn about the issues (from women's groups, books, labor de-partments of government, trade unions).
• If you belong to a union, encourage it to treat women equally and to fight for equal-pay clauses, maternity leave, equal job oppor-tunities and fairer benefit packages (which might include such aids as day-care facilities).
• Persistence might gain you entrance to higher-paying "male" jobs through retraining schemes. See your local government employ-ment office or a trade school about how to become a bricklayer, a telephone linewoman, a truck driver or a plumber. Even with gov-ernment-sponsored affirmative-action programs, you have to be determined to gain entrance to and acceptance in such high-pay fields. You won't meet less prejudice; in fact, as the sole woman in a construction gang you may receive an even rougher time. But if you persist, at least you'll be well paid. According to the United States Bureau of Labor, by 1985, 80 percent of all jobs will require speciali-zed training, yet only 20 percent will require college.
• Employ yourself: despite running a house and raising children

single-handedly, many a single mother has developed her own business. You might even do this from your home. The glitter of self-satisfaction in the eyes of a West Coast single mother who started by selling gift items on commission and who now owns a chain of five gift shops is matched only by the pride in the eyes of her daughters:

I started literally with a suitcase, my daughters and the need to feed us and pay the hotel bill after we arrived in this city. I knew I could do it — because I had to.

And she did it in less than three years.

LEGAL

There are two aspects to the potential prejudice that single parents face in the field of law: the legal system itself and its practitioners.

The legal system's basic concern with private ownership (until quite recently women were considered the property of their fathers or husbands) and its emphasis on the adversary approach have spelled misery for hundreds of parents and children. Who is entitled to how much? The adversary system pits wife against husband, child against parent (an illegitimate child claiming an inheritance, for example). "Rights" often seem to be interpreted in the narrow sense of monetary claims and only secondarily, or not at all, in the broader sense of human dignity.

As if this were not enough, lawyers often reflect prejudice in society at large in discriminating against single fathers in some ways and against single mothers in others.

Lawyers are scavengers on people like me. They think women are predominantly emotional and stupid, especially in divorce cases. My first lawyer urged me to buy, buy. So I did. But he had misled me. I was sued, my ex didn't have to pay and I was judged against. My wages were garnisheed.

Boy! Did I have bad advice from my first lawyer. Because of him I ended up being accused of deserting the children. In my ignorance, I had even signed over custody on that lawyer's advice.

You've got to trust your lawyer, but they're all out for the buck. My third lawyer has just told me she can't continue the case because last month's bill alone, which I can't pay, is $3,000. To me, that's blackmail.

Many a divorcée has been branded as unfit to retain custody of her children, not because she abused them but because her moral behavior was not as impeccable as the court desired. Has a sexually-active single father ever been so condemned? Not that fathers fare well before the law. Many fathers are hurt by the reluctance of most judges to entrust young children, especially girls, to their care. And many complain of being forced to pay steep support or of being denied sufficient access to their children.

There has been an automatic presumption that a child is better off in the custody of its mother. There is as little evidence to support this view as there is to support the opposite. Common sense would dictate that a child should, if at all possible, be placed in the custody of both its parents. (If one of the parents and the child really can't get along, or if one parent is a child abuser, then the physical part of joint custody is not feasible.) Support payments should be for the children, not the ex-spouse, and mothers should be as liable for financial support of children living with their father as is now the case in reverse.

Pressure from single-parent organizations, enlightened lawyers and other professionals is gradually bringing about change. Eight states are actually putting the child's interests first by encouraging joint custody. Several provinces now recognize that marriage is an economic partnership; when the partnership dissolves, the wife— even if she "only" stayed home and reared the children—is entitled to a sizeable share of the family assets. (But as Lynn King says in her book *What Every Woman Should Know About Marriage, Separation and Divorce*, "Although we now have all sorts of family legislation that makes claims to equality, women learn only too late that these are mostly just words.") Family courts—where the child is listened to, too—are being established to resolve child-custody agreements away from the triallike atmosphere of traditional court battles. And, as more and more fathers sue for custody (and some for support payments, too), judges are beginning to face the fact that men can, and want, to parent.

Deciding what is best for a particular child in a particular situation is not easy. Beyond the obvious criteria of physical neglect or abuse, who can say what is good parenting or a good environment? Raising children is not as simple as selecting a car. To a large extent, social pressures, which change from one era to another, decide who will be the better parent or whether both should have equal rights and responsibilities for the child, which is why judges are turning increasingly toward mental health professionals such as social workers and psychiatrists for help in deciding custody. Although the "science" of such professionals is far from exact, their advice seems to work in Los Angeles. Therapists there successfully mediate 55 percent of the cases (and one in five disputes ends in a plan for joint custody). In Wisconsin—where the law requires that a lawyer be appointed to represent the child if the parents are fighting over custody— a lawyer, rather than a social worker, interviews neighbors, friends, clergy and teachers for guidance about which living arrangement is best for the child.

Although it is preferable to settle out of court if at all possible, the adversary system *is* effective when all hope of calm, rational settlement is lost—when one partner is hiding financial assets or otherwise not acting in good faith. If the relationship is going to be sour anyway, the children need to get what they are entitled to. For that, a tough lawyer on their side in the adversary battle is best.

Another area in which a lawyer can be very useful is that of your will. Although you can draw up your own will (details vary from place to place), legal advice might well be necessary if you want to be sure your children receive whatever material goods you can leave them. This is especially important for the children of never-married mothers, because in many jurisdictions an illegitimate child has no right to inherit from his mother—unless she has named him in her will.

Some parents choose not to burden their children with a funeral. They prefer to donate their bodies to medical research and to the enriching of someone else's life or sight through a transplant of a kidney or an eye. (Contact your local hospital or Kidney Foundation for information. In some areas, you may simply sign on a special line on your driving licence.) Another important consideration is who you want to have custody of your children should you die before they are grown. This, and your wishes regarding the disposal of your body, should be made clear, verbally and in writing, with responsible people and with a lawyer, now. One single father, deserted by his wife three years before had been unaware how anxious his child was about the possibility of his death:

I was surprised when Michelle (six years old) asked "What happens to me if you die?" It must really have bothered her because she kept asking me.

At first, I shrugged off the question, telling her not to worry. I would be around for a long time and probably wouldn't die until she was well grown up. But one day she came home from school bawling because one of the kids in her class had told her his father had died on the weekend. (He was a policeman killed in a traffic accident.) Wow! That made me realize that I had to comfort Michelle, but also I had to make some realistic plans in case I do die before she grows up.

Both of us feel better now I've arranged for her to live with my brother and his wife if the worst happens. Also, I took out a life-insurance policy so that she'll at least have a little money. It sure was a weight off my mind once I made definite plans for her. I think my feeling good about it—not that I really feel it's real that I'm going to die—helped Michelle, too.

A free booklet, *Knowing*, in which you can record the location of bank accounts, important papers, names of legal advisers, burial wishes, etc., is available from Chartered Life Underwriters (41 Lesmill Road, Don Mills, Ontario, Canada M3B 2T3).

How can you find a dependable lawyer? One compassionate member of the legal profession, himself the son of a single parent, suggests the following:

• Check with your friends or single-parent organization: word of mouth is one of the best ways to find a trustworthy lawyer. However, a lawyer who is suitable even to your closest friend may still not be right for you. When a friend or business associate recommends a lawyer, ask the three key questions: Was the lawyer reliable? Were you kept informed? Were the costs fair?
• Sit in on a few cases to see lawyers in action.
• Call your nearest bar association for names of lawyers who handle separation and divorce cases (bar associations are listed in the White Pages).
• If you know or have heard of someone with a style you like in a related profession (such as accounting or stockbrokering), ask that person for the name of a good lawyer.
• Put together all the documents you might need so that you are well armed at the first visit and don't have to waste time and money for a follow-up meeting. Take along such things as birth certificates, marriage contracts, names and addresses of witnesses, marriage certificate, police reports, social agency records, proof of earnings or financial transactions between you and your spouse.
• Always ask the cost of talking with a lawyer before you settle down for a discussion.
• If you're short of cash, find out if you're eligible for legal aid by tele-

phoning your local Legal Aid Association. If you can't find it, call the bar association or any legal office (listed in the Yellow Pages). In some areas, although *you* may be poor, if your ex is rich, you may not be entitled to legal aid. However, there may be a provision in your provincial or state law that allows the court to require your rich ex to cover court costs.

• Know something about your rights before you meet a lawyer. Don't rely on hearsay or what happened to your second cousin twice-removed. Read a plain-language family law book. Since it is essential that the book be up to date, ask your librarian or bookseller to check for the latest one that applies to where you live. Such a book will prime you with the kind of questions you may not have thought of, and suggest answers to some of your legal worries. Perhaps the justice department publishes handbooks explaining the law simply. In Canada, a listing of all such booklets put out by each province is available in the *Canadian Community Law Journal* (University of Windsor, Faculty of Law, Windsor, Ontario N9B 3P4).

• Don't expect anything for free. The lawyer charges for his or her time, and that includes phone calls. Keep your calls to a minimum, and essential.

• Have legal fees put in writing. An honest lawyer will have no objection to sending or giving you a letter spelling out the service he or she has agreed to provide and the actual or estimated charges. If the costs won't be known completely until after the case is over, then the lawyer should write down the method that will be used to arrive at the final cost. This letter is important because it will help to avoid misunderstandings and enable you to plan in advance for payment.

• Bargain over fixed fees. If you think your case is straightforward and does not justify the use of a fixed-schedule fee (set in some areas by the local bar), then suggest a lower fee or an hourly rate.

• Always read a document carefully before you sign it; be sure you understand everything. (For example, the parent who makes support payments can deduct these from his or her income tax; the one who receives the money has to declare it as income.)

• If anything new happens, tell the lawyer immediately. (You can always dictate a message to the lawyer's secretary if the lawyer is busy.) One single mother was so distraught by the accidental death of her daughter that she neglected to tell the lawyer, and ended up having to pay him for his time spent preparing for a custody battle that would never be fought.

Here's what to find out when you meet a lawyer:

- Is he or she really interested in your case? Does the lawyer behave as though this is simply routine, or is he or she listening carefully?
- Is the lawyer willing to try to get everything settled out of court? Some extra effort by the lawyer might achieve a settlement without an expensive, ugly court battle.
- Is the lawyer prepared to handle the case according to the kind of relationship you have with the other parent? No two situations are exactly alike: sometimes a friendly, even trusting, atmosphere exists between the former marital partners (especially regarding the children) and all that is needed is a legalizing of the separation. In other relationships, a single parent may feel his or her children are entitled to more money than the ex-spouse appears willing to pay.
- How do you feel about this lawyer? Do you get the impression that his or her main concern is what will be best for the children? (The lawyer quoted earlier advises that parents look past their own pride and desire for revenge to put the children's interests first.)
- Is separation and divorce the lawyer's specialty? There's little point in consulting a lawyer who works full-time on corporation deals.
- When can you reach the lawyer? You must know how accessible your lawyer will be. Does she spend most of her time in court? Does he see clients by appointment only? Can you chat on the phone with the lawyer?
- How long has the lawyer been in practice? Whether you want a fresh lawyer or one with lots of experience will depend on your preferences and the nature of your case. A young lawyer may charge less and be eager to take on the world on your behalf; a more experienced lawyer may be more effective in the courtroom, or too jaded to care.
- How will the lawyer bill you? This is extremely important. You should be very clear if you are going to pay by the hour, by a retainer or by some other method. Also, find out what the charges are for a telephone call, a letter and each of the other standard expenses. Insist on a written list of the lawyer's fees and an itemized bill.
- Will the lawyer be handling your case or referring it to someone else? If the lawyer you are interviewing is going to hand the case over to a person you haven't met, you have the choice of refusing, interviewing the junior colleague or insisting that the supervising lawyer keep accurate control of the case and be available to you.

Also, make sure you are not paying a partner's fees for a student's work.
• Will the lawyer keep you informed (in plain language) about how the case is going? How long will it take? What are your chances of getting what you want?

SCHOOLS

Schools are sometimes the worst offenders against single parents. Teachers tend to stereotype the family: they ask children to draw little pictures of mummy and daddy and brothers and sisters outside the house. In this case, it is often single fathers who feel it most.

My children came home and said, "We told the teacher there's no mummy in our house, but she wouldn't believe us. She said we must have a mummy and we said no, we don't." The other kids in the class found that odd and some told mine, "I've got a mummy but no daddy."

Teachers, despite school records, will ask for "Mrs." when they telephone. Many textbooks are still not only sexist but also typecast: there is a daddy and a mummy and each has assigned roles. This confuses the child who knows his single parent combines all the roles.

A small child faces discrimination early. He or she will bring home paintings and cards from kindergarten addressed to "Mummy and Daddy" at Christmas and Mother's and Father's Day respectively. (Ironically, Father's Day was begun by a woman as a tribute to her single father.)

New York State has workshops for teachers and school psychologists counseling children of single-parent families. Such programs should be introduced elsewhere, providing they are established as resources, not role-setters. Advice, help or encouragement from teachers should be available to single-parent families that want it. But there should be a keen awareness that not every child of every single parent will have problems at school. It's sensitivity that's required, not censuring. Otherwise, the school may go from the extreme of paying no attention to the different life-situation of our children to expecting trouble. (Expecting to see unhealthy families instead of single-parent families that are doing well.)

A single parent can do several things about prejudice in schools. First, get involved. Your interaction with your child's teachers can immensely improve the situation for you, the teacher, your child and single-parent families in general. A teacher alerted, in advance, about Mother's and Father's Day for instance, can take appropriate steps.

"Make it clear that the issue of single parenthood is broader than just your own child," advises a single mother of two grade-school children. This kind of awareness is very important. It was overlooked by Alison, perhaps because she has a live-in sitter:

At my children's school last year, parents were discussing the withdrawal of children from school as a method for us to demonstrate support for the teacher's sporadic strikes. I'm sorry to say I was not the one who pointed out that we would have to make arrangements for the single-parent families, most of whom need somewhere safe and sure for their children during the day.

Examine your child's textbooks for sexism and a bias in favor of stereotyped coupled families. When you discover such anachronisms, let the teacher, parents' committee, principal and school board know. Perhaps you could suggest more relevant texts. It would be very helpful for teachers, parents and children alike to have texts that portray enjoyable single-parent homes. This is urgent in both affluent suburban and poverty-stricken inner city schools. Children from single-parent homes make up 20 to 80 percent of a school's population.

Some children are so resilient that their single-parent status doesn't embarrass them; others find comfort in numbers. But many suffer from feeling different. Here's what to do to help your child:

• Be active. Opportunities to discuss something that bothers your child will arise naturally as you discuss homework, visit the school or volunteer for parent/school activities. Know, and prime, the teachers. Involved single parents may be able to set up after-school programs, which can be of enormous benefit to both child and parent.
• Do not make an issue of single parenthood. If you sit down for an earnest chat about the prejudice your child may face at school you're likely to alarm her unduly—and alert your child to look for slights. Although many schools are tough on single-parent children, some are not. In a few, the trend is even the other way. Thirteen-year-old Eva came home from school one day and told her

father (who has raised her since she was three): "Quite a few of my friends say they wish their parents would separate."
- Buy or borrow suitable pro-single-parent books for your child. Read along with her, if she's very young.
- Draw your child's attention to positive single-parent homes—either real ones that you know, or those on television or in the movies.
- Tell your child about famous or talented people whose parents were single (Leonardo da Vinci and Jean-Paul Sartre, for example).
- Don't hesitate to mention the good aspects of being a single parent. A single father can be proud of the cakes he's made for the school bake sale; a single mother may point out she's the only mother in the whole school to know major-league baseball inside out—things they were not likely to have done if they weren't single parents.
- Answer your child's questions—immediately. When he wants to know why you're not married, tell him. Naturally, your answer has to be in tune with what you show the child. It's harmful to say, for example, "I'm happier on my own, with you," if he sees you moping around miserably.
- Correct misconceptions. A child from a single-parent home will often pick up inappropriate ideas at school. For example, one ten-year-old boy refused to do what his separated father asked. "No, pop, I don't do dishes, I'm a man." The refusal gave the father an excellent chance to explain how single parents do all the chores and work outside the home, but that this doesn't make them any less a man (or woman).

MEDIA

There is a tendency in the media to present the negative. Thus single parents are frequently portrayed as miserable, unfulfilled and lonely. Commendable exceptions to this negative emphasis were several articles in the late seventies in the *Toronto Star* and the Montreal *Gazette*. Single parents and their children spoke of their new happiness. While not glossing over difficulties, they elaborated on the advantages they had discovered in single parenthood.

Such articles and the increasing number of similar programs on television or radio should be praised. If you drop a postcard or a letter or telephone the respective editors, you will feel good and you will enhance the image of all single parents. Similarly, negative stereotypes should be protested against.

There are other actions you can take concerning the media. You can let bookstores, libraries and magazine and book publishers know that you want material, especially for children, that present the single-parent family as the healthy, normal and even superior arrangement that it can be. You can buy single-parent books. You might even write one. And more than one single parent has begun a column in a local paper.

LANGUAGE

Demeaning and stereotyped language is very damaging to the cause of single parents. Regardless of the contrary evidence, sociologists refer to single-parent families as "culturally deprived" and "pathogenic." Such mythmakers, evidently unaware of their own biases, assume that the absence of one parent—especially if that parent is male—automatically leads to social sickness. They are rarely interested in healthy, happy single-parent homes. Families headed by women are not referred to as "mother-led," but as "father-absent," defining the situation negatively—and from a male perspective. A never-married mother began to believe there was something wrong with her, because the social worker said she was an "incomplete personality." When the single mother realized that this was just a prejudice of the social worker, she stopped blaming herself. The labels blind social workers and others, including single parents, who absorb the disparaging attitudes. For example, one single parent, a teacher, frequently refers to us as "split families," and another single mother, who wrote a book of advice, calls us "half families."

Sexist language and attitudes particularly hurt single parents. A single mother recalls how restricted her thinking used to be:

I remember begging my husband to take out the garbage. That was "the man's job." I was working as an executive secretary. At home, I did the cleaning, shopping, cooking, washing and ironing. I attended PTA meetings and drove the kids to the doctor. The least my husband could do was fulfill the man's work!

The myth of "men's work" and "women's work" is shattered by the existence of the single-parent family. You indicate by behavior, and should also do so through language, that chores, jobs and careers are not related to gender. "The more a single parent desexes language, the more single-parent status is enhanced," says one single parent. Changing language biases means changing the way we think about ourselves.

SOCIAL

Ruth is a never-married, low-income mother and one of many single parents who are angry at being mistreated socially:

I know how I feel as a woman and as a mother. I know I love my daughter just as much as anyone who is married. I know I am just as responsible with my child. And I feel it is unfair because of my marital status or my economic condition and the problems I face, that I am being dragged in the mud.

Caroline, who had left her husband six months previously, describes a reaction common to many recently separated single mothers:

Socially, I've found being an odd woman quite difficult. It starts to get to you after a while. Friends don't even think of inviting me—married friends, that is. Even my parents won't accept the fact that I'm separated. None of my four older sisters will visit me now that I'm on my own.

And Graham was surprised, soon after his separation became general knowledge, that "the neighbors across the street would no longer allow my kids to use their private swimming pool."

No wonder single parents become angry at such social slights. What can you do when this happens to you? Don't bottle it up, or, worse, pour it out on your children—direct your anger at the persons responsible.

When the social stigma comes from "friends," the solution is clear: drop them and create a new network. (See Chapter 3 on overcoming loneliness.) Relatives may change their minds after a period of time, especially if they are your parents. They'll probably want to see the grandchild eventually, so keep in contact. When a reunion is planned, try to keep it casual: avoid having it on an emotionally significant holiday, for example. Expectations and tensions are too high at times such as Christmas. Reconciliations are easier afterward, in the guilty wake of a family time not celebrated.

CREDIT

It is mostly single mothers, rather than fathers, that meet discrimination in trying to obtain loans or financing. Practice still lags behind the law, as this single mother testifies:

I could have got a mortgage much more easily with my ex's signature (he was willing to sign), but I stuck it out and insisted to the bank that I wanted the mortgage in my name only. I finally got it. It helped to have a female real-estate agent who was herself a single parent. She understood exactly how I felt, whereas the man in the mortgage department didn't understand why I wanted to do it the hard way.

A single mother has to be firm and persistent, a single father writes:

We'd been separated about eight months when my ex called and tearfully pleaded with me to co-sign a bank loan for a car for her. The loan officer had flatly refused to give her a loan unless she had a man co-sign. I told her she was on her own now, I wasn't going to sign anything, and there was no reason that the bank should refuse her the money. She had a good job and they always have the car as collateral. She went back, argued with the loan officer, threatened him with adverse publicity if he continued to discriminate against her, and got the loan.

If a woman wants credit, she has to establish a rating in her own name. If, before becoming a single parent, you were married, it is possible you do not have a rating distinct from that of your ex-husband. Now that you are on your own, credit might be useful. How can you qualify? To get credit, you need a credit history—a file showing your purchases and payments on credit. A simple way to begin is to apply for one of the major credit cards or a department store card. (Almost anyone can qualify.) Have it issued in your own name (Mary Jones) not your husband's (Mrs. John Jones). As you make your ordinary purchases and pay for them, you will build a credit rating. This, in turn, will help you to get credit elsewhere, because every potential credit-giver checks your credit-worthiness with the local consumer-credit reporting agency.

I have a driver's licence, but I don't have a car. I applied for a credit card from one of the oil companies. When a friend takes me and my daughter for a drive, I use the card to get the tank filled up with gas. The friend often pays me half the bill—in cash. I pay the oil company promptly when the bill comes in a month or so later. This way I built a credit file very easily, since we go out two or three times a month.

Another easy method for establishing credit is to borrow from yourself. If you have a savings account (or bonds or savings certificates) worth, say, $600, borrow $600 against the account for five or six months. The bank or credit union will freeze your savings until the loan is paid off. Since the charge for this will usually be only 1 or 2 percent more than the annual interest on the savings account, you are establishing a credit record quite cheaply.

Secured credit, such as a car loan, is usually easier to obtain, providing you can produce evidence of ASA; not the medicine, but Ability, Stability and Alacrity:

- Your *ability* to pay depends on your income, your present and future obligations, and your expected income.
- Your *stability* includes such things as how long you've held your present job, lived in the same neighborhood, whether or not you own your own home, have a telephone and a bank account.
- Your *alacrity* means how willing you have been to repay debts—and this is revealed in your credit history.

Single mothers in the United States should remember these points about the Equal Credit Opportunity Act: a creditor—

- is required by the law to explain why you were refused credit.
- may *not* discriminate against you because you are single, or because you are a woman.
- may *not* demand information about your birth-control behavior, childbearing capabilities or intentions.
- may *not* require a cosignatory on a loan unless it is required from all similarly qualified applicants, both male and female, married and unmarried.
- must consider alimony and child-support payments just as any other source of income would be considered, if you so request.

WELFARE

Far from worrying about being granted credit, many single parents are desperately trying to manage on welfare. Between a third and a half of all single mothers turn to welfare, at least for a while. Single fathers meet another discrimination: they are usually not even allowed the "choice" of going on welfare.

"Ontario Family Benefits discriminate against single fathers," noted Robert Cooper, the former Canadian television ombudsman. He pointed out that only thirteen fathers have received such social aid in Ontario—by special dispensation. To date, there has been no change in the law.

Alberta, British Columbia and the United States claim to have eliminated sex discrimination from the welfare system. In Quebec, the Social Aid law is explicit on the right to aid if you are "alone to take care of a child under six years of age." Yet an official of the social affairs department in Montreal expressed her horror at the idea of a single father staying home with his preschool child. She said the only circumstances under which a single father could get welfare would be if he were very sick—and even that would be short-term.

This is grossly unfair. If it would be better for a single father to be at home with his family, he, just as much as a single mother, should have that choice. So ingrained is the "man must work" concept that even a single father will believe that work outside the home is more essential to his well-being and dignity than is such work for a woman.

For single mothers, the bitter irony is that one prejudice of society —that women belong at home—is compounded by another: that no one should get something for nothing. So, welfare rates are kept at or below the minimum necessary for survival. This is to encourage recipients to go out to work. Yet the majority of persons receiving welfare are mothers doing their best to hold their families together. Many single mothers are untrained for all but the most menial, low-paying jobs. If they do work outside the home, they can't earn enough to pay for adequate child care. Either way—on welfare or at work but away from the children—society frowns upon the single mother. Meanwhile, the children suffer from the shame, guilt and anxiety imposed on thousands of single mothers every year. Most of our social services are concerned with patching up, rather than preventing, human tragedy. The welfare system barely admits how important the work of a single parent is in maintaining a home and raising her children.

Welfare for a single mother is often worse than marriage. The state dictates the single mother's morality, oversees her private life. A mother treated as incompetent, lazy and immoral must fight hard to prevent these attitudes from becoming part of her self-image.

HOW TO APPROACH THE WELFARE OFFICE

First, keep in mind that if you have no other substantial income you have a *right* to welfare (called social aid in some parts of Canada, and Aid to Families with Dependent Children—AFDC—in the United States). Welfare programs are there to share a little of the general wealth (to which you have contributed) with families facing serious hardship.

It's an unusual welfare office that is cheery and welcoming. The apparent indifference, even hostility of some welfare workers may be caused by their despair at the constant litany of human tragedies and problems they hear every day, all day—and the inadequate tools given them to drain this morass of misery.

- Phone for an appointment (look in the telephone book under provincial or state services); ask what documents you should bring.
- At the office you may have a long, tedious wait. Be prepared: knit, sew, read, write letters, chat with other applicants. Do not bring your children unless you must. If you do, keep them occupied constructively (coloring books, playing word games, reading).
- If possible, bring a friend or a welfare-rights advocate with you. (Welfare-rights groups are not as plentiful as they were in the late sixties, but there may be one in your district: check with a church or social agency. There may be a group like Toronto's MOM—Mothers Organizing Mothers—near you.) A friend or a knowledgeable person will help to make sure you get all the assistance you're entitled to, and can be useful as a witness if you have to appeal a decision or lay a complaint.
- Bring all the papers you think might be asked for (such as birth certificates, rent receipts, proof of debts, marriage licence, court separation or divorce papers, affidavits from social workers, utility bills, medical bills, bank book, eviction notice, income-tax return,

citizenship papers, firing notice). Offer the interviewer only the documents he or she specifically asks for.

- During the interview, keep calm. Look cool on the outside even if you're quaking on the inside. Be dignified but not arrogant. Speak quietly but firmly.

- Go along with the form-filling, apparently stupid questions and other routines (unless the interviewer makes suggestive or illegal remarks).

- Ask the welfare worker's name. Use it. Establish further rapport: show you understand that the bureaucrat's job is tough.

- Encourage him or her to talk. (This may lead to information about your rights that you wouldn't otherwise receive.)

- Never volunteer information. You'll be asked everything necessary.

- Get as much documentation as possible before and during the interview (such as payment schedules, eligibility requirements, rights to such things as medical payments, education while still receiving welfare, etc.) If possible, get a copy of the law covering social assistance in your area. How? Ask.

- If you are dissatisfied, ask to see the worker's superior. Inquire about appeal procedures. At this point, don't be bashful: you and your children have to eat.

- Always be sure you've clearly understood everything. If you have an ex, is that person obligated to support you and did you sign an agreement for the authorities to press charges? How much are you legally allowed to earn before your welfare money is reduced?

Some pointers for those receiving welfare:

- Find out if your welfare department will help you move to a small community just outside a large center: this probably will improve your living conditions immensely. In addition to fresh air and country space for the children, rents are usually lower: the money that welfare would allow for rent in the city will provide a more roomy dwelling in the country.

- Earn whatever extra income you can from baby-sitting, typing, housecleaning or whatever. There is a limit to the amount of such income allowed, after which your payments are reduced.

- Get to know your neighbors. It's good for your morale for you to be known to your neighbors as a clean, responsible person and a loving mother. A woman alone on welfare often has need of friendly neighbors—they'll keep an eye on your child while she's playing and you're doing the wash, for example; they'll not be spiteful if a welfare investigator asks questions about you.

- Pay your rent (if it's not paid directly by the welfare department) as soon as your check arrives, but don't splurge the rest. This awful temptation has led many single mothers into horrible messes. At the end of the month, with all the money gone and the children hungry, you may feel forced to borrow money you can never pay back in cash. So, if there is a convenient bank or credit union nearby, deposit your check in a no-charge checking account or a daily interest savings account. Pay yourself a portion of the money each week. Or, cash your check and split the money into four envelopes; put slightly more than a quarter of the total in the fourth envelope (you're paid once a month but each calendar month has about four and one-half weeks).
- Budget carefully: you have a small amount of money to be stretched a long way. Read the money-saving tips on pages 60-63, and ask your welfare worker if the department has further budgeting advice. Check your local library and women's groups for more.
- Be prepared for an investigation. You don't have to be a fanatic about house cleaning, but if your home is tidy it will immediately make a good impression. Welfare workers are supposed to visit every recipient's home, but some single mothers don't see a worker for years. If the investigator is male, arrange a "come-quick-I-need-you" signal beforehand with a neighbor or leave the front door open. Never let boyfriends leave articles of male clothing or toiletries—in many states and provinces, evidence of a live-in man is sufficient to have you cut off welfare.
- Plan ahead: draw up a plan for your future. Aim at returning to school or work when the children are old enough. Such a plan helps you to survive the difficult, lean years on welfare.
- Receive the maximum benefits you are entitled to. That's not just the monthly allowance. In your province or state there may be free dental care for the children, reduced rates on prescribed drugs, transportation discounts, food stamps. Welfare departments sometimes save money by conveniently overlooking some of the benefits they should be paying out. Find out from social workers, other single mothers, women's groups or the law itself what you can collect. Before going off welfare, be sure to use these benefits to the full (for example, free glasses if your child needs them).

- Use your time constructively: the worst you can do for yourself, your child and single mothers in general, is to pass day after dreary day in front of the television, smoking in boredom. Get out, especially with your child.

I really enjoy this life. Money is short—very short—but my daughter and I go so many places, do so many things together. I take her to all the free activities, like the museum, art gallery, dramas on the stage in the park, swimming. I've joined so many activities at the community center that people think I'm one of the staff. I've learned to make pottery, play the guitar, weave, speak Spanish and cook better. The most fun is the folk dancing. We're also busy in church doings so that means picnics and lectures and Sunday school outings and cross-country skiing. I even get to the movies—'course, they're a bit old, I see them at the Repertory Theatre for $1.99, and at the University for $2.50. A single mother just down the street looks after my daughter, and I do the same for her when she wants someone to look after her little boy. He comes over here and sometimes stays the night. It gives her a break and time to be with her boyfriend. Next year, I think I'll take a woodworking course.

- Join, or start, a single-mothers group. Such a group can be therapy for a single mother bewildered and upset by the situation she's in, or, like MOMMA was in the United States, it can be a movement for change in welfare laws and attitudes.
- Eat healthily: it's easy to be depressed if you are not eating well. Welfare money won't permit many steaks, but now is your chance to learn what food is comparatively cheap, yet nutritious. Ask at your local library for books on nutrition. You and your child will be glad you did. A family of five can eat adequately for less than two dollars a day (in 1980), according to the Montreal Diet Dispensary which has offered nutrition counseling to single parents for over 100 years.
- Learn money-saving skills. Take a community center course or ask a friend to teach you how to fix small appliances, do simple plumbing and make or adapt your own clothes.
- Escape the welfare treadmill by attending school while you collect. Some places forbid this. In other jurisdictions, government loans and bursaries are available to single mothers who wish to earn a certificate or a diploma and use their training to begin a career. Your welfare department or adult-education authority will know what your local regulations are. Check the legal provisions yourself, because this is often the kind of unusual thing that a particular worker

may never have heard of. In Ontario, several hundred single mothers on welfare are attending college thanks to student grants, which cover textbooks, sitters, fees, etc.

Single parents who refuse to be crushed by the degrading welfare system are a testimonial to human dignity.

DAY CARE

It is not so much that single parents meet prejudice in day-care centers, but that there is not enough day care, public or private. And this hurts single parents more, since they don't have the alternative of a spouse to look after the children. Many single parents *must* work outside the home. The few who can afford it pay for care in commercial centers or private homes. Some have relatives with the time and energy to devote to the children. But the majority is forced to make inconvenient, haphazard, even dangerous arrangements, which in turn often means having to give up a job.

The average yearly salary of a woman in the United States in 1979 was $8,000—obviously not enough for a sole-support mother to afford adequate private day care. The number of working mothers in the United States—over 40 percent of them single—is expected to double, to twelve million, by 1985, yet there is no comprehensive government policy on day care. The situation in Canada is no better: in Ontario there are more than two hundred thousand children under five whose mothers go out to work, but only fifty-three thousand spaces available in licensed day-care centers. It's hard enough for a single parent to manage financially, but how is a sole-support mother to pay for day care when her average wage is 40 percent lower than the average man's salary?

The shortage of day care continues because it is not seen as a responsibility of men. "Governments are afraid of the words day care," says Lynne Gordon, chairperson of the Ontario Status of Women Council. More than ordinary day care is required.

We need subsidized, licensed day-care homes, after-school centers, emergency short-term centers, industrial and corporate-based centers and mobile day-care buses for rural areas—all as official parts of government employment strategy.

The bias against women being in the work force lets government ignore day care, causing painful psychological or physical results for children left on their own or in the care of untrained people. In 1971, the United States Congress approved the spending of fifteen billion dollars to provide "quality child care" on a large scale. Then-President Richard Nixon vetoed the bill, claiming that family life would be threatened by such government interference. Every comprehensive day-care bill since then has been defeated by conservative representatives who believe a woman's place is at home minding the children. Lynne Gordon makes it clear that

when governments and business truly believe women have the right to belong to the primary work force—not just for pin money, but for keeps—then they will provide adequate day care for working parents.

Day care should not be seen only in the narrow light of freeing mothers to work outside the home. A day-care center will have a big influence on a child's values and sense of self-esteem. It should be a place for the child to learn healthy ways of getting along with people, discovering himself and enlarging his world. Some centers are more concerned with institutional efficiency or peace and quiet for the staff. Such places, where your child is going to be inhibited all day or even encouraged to sleep all afternoon, are going to instill a negative image in his mind, and make him explosive at night as he lets off the steam that has been bottled up during the day. This can be extremely hard on a parent who, after a full working day, has to cope with the aggression without the support of another adult.

Where good day care is available at a reasonable price, the benefits for children and parents are enormous. A unique service, operating twenty-four hours a day, is the Forbid Them Not Children's Centre and its companion A New Life Centre in Hamilton, Ontario. In a homelike atmosphere, these centers enhance the preschoolers' development. Parents participate in decision making and in the running of the centers. Parents also receive individual and group guidance in raising their children. Single father Len is able to work odd shifts in a car factory and single mother Irma can start work as a letter carrier at 6:00 A.M., both confident that their children are being well cared for.

Family day care is also a solution for the single parent. This is quality care of a limited number of children in a private home. There are probably a lot of people—including single parents—now subsisting on welfare who would relish being trained in the group care of children and who could be employed in homes or in extra-school programs. This would free many others to work, and up-grade or otherwise fulfill themselves.

Until governments and business change their attitudes, some single parents are getting together (sometimes with coupled fami-lies) to create their own day-care centers. The costs, though, with-out government subsidies often prove disastrous. Sometimes governments can be persuaded to provide help through cash grants or loans of buildings. Then the parents are able to go beyond the "parking-lot mentality" that so annoys thirty-three-year-old Nadine, a single mother very much involved in parent-run day care:

Parent-run day care is geared to be a service for the benefit of the children. Which is why there is a ratio of one monitor to seven children. They can take the children out, they can do things with them.

In contrast, that's why most private day cares have a back yard: they can't take the kids anywhere. There are too many kids to take.

Government norms are unrealistic. They feel that one person can look after fifteen children adequately. A day care is a place that you dump your kids from nine to five, and that's it. Most have no idea what day care is, what it could be, what it should be. Their attitude is that day care is a park-ing lot. Somewhere to park your kids for the day. Private day cares *are* parking lots. You don't expect anything fantastic to come out of them.

Parent-run day care is better because I like the ratio, I like the fact that I pay $10 a week for my child. She gets lunch, she gets two snacks. I know she's out during the day at least once. She's learning French and she's very fond of the people there.

I know every day at what time she's doing what because I help make the schedule. I can walk into that day care and, in a meeting, I can say what I like and don't like. I have some control over what goes on there.

Before putting your child in any kind of day care, check the place out personally, talk with other parents and the staff. Be wary of a center that won't allow you to see it in operation.

Day care should be a community service, as normal as public education. Children should be admitted solely on the basis of their readiness. The prime purpose of day care should be the *well* fare of the children. In the meantime, single parents such as Nadine will continue to fight for small-scale, humanistic day care controlled by parents. It will be a long battle to achieve universal day care. The struggle is intertwined with all the other prejudices single parents face.

FIGHT PREJUDICE
AND DISCRIMINATION

A family striving alone is often unaware of the social causes and implications of its situation. Ultimate freedom from prejudice and discrimination will come when single parents are no longer a designated group; when we will have shown by our lives that ours is a valid, acceptable choice of lifestyle. Ultimately, each single parent family is an ambassador.

SEVEN

SEX
AND
THE SINGLE PARENT

THE SEXUAL HABITS OF SINGLE PARENTS
vary as much as the individuals. Some newly
separated single parents go on a kind of spree; others attempt to,
but find it difficult to put the desire into practice; and some just
remain celibate. Most single parents are extremely wary—a caution
that is part self-uncertainty and part suspicion—but which seems to
be relatively persistent over the years.

There is a lot of confusion at first. Henry, suddenly alone at
thirty-two with two sons and a daughter, found himself asking a lot
of questions:

You're single again. You try to prove something. Even though you are a lot
older, you tend to think you are twenty-one. But you are not, you're a lot
more complex. It was hard to ask myself all those horrible questions I
avoided before. Like what am I expecting from women? And am I a chauvinist?

It's a maturing process in that it's facing relationships with thirty-year-
olds. Most of these women have hurt feelings too. A lot of people are hurt,
messed up. It's hurt talking to hurt. Your expectations and fears are
greater.

At the same time, you know certain things for sure: you are a package
deal, you have three kids. You can't promise anything and yet you feel you
should.

SELF-INDULGENCE
OR SELF-DENIAL

For single fathers, heterosexual experiences seem to come in abun-
dance, or rarely; the single father either finds himself surrounded
by available, eager women or he seems to be in a sexual desert.

Some women are attracted by a single father's situation. They admire him for "being able to cope." As Bert, single father of a seven-year-old boy, observes:

Being a single father has enhanced my status. Many women feel like mothering my child and me, too. I take full advantage of it.

Other separated single fathers find it hard to know how to behave with women. There is a feeling of emptiness—what Desmond calls "the void"—following the separation.

The void lasts a long time, because it becomes reinforced when you try to relate to women. Most complain that you are controlling or insecure or unassertive. You feel close to a person, yet far away. Somehow the intimacy is short-lived. I began to think there was something wrong with me because women were being so critical of me.

In some cases, the single parents have been so hurt by bad experiences that they hesitate to get involved with another person. In other cases, they find that they do not need intercourse with the opposite sex. After "a year of whoring around," Rebecca woke up to another attitude and has refrained from sex ever since:

I am one of those kind of people that going to bed with someone when I'm not married really gets to me. So here I am. I don't know what I'm going to do for the rest of my days. I've just found that . . . because of the way I think about sex, I'm better off to be without it than to go ahead and be with it. I spoke to a professional and said that one of the things that bothers me most is not "doing without sex," it's people trying to coerce me or convince me that it's impossible to live my life without it. You know, "There's no way, you're only human." And she said, "That's really the whole point: you are human. You can make a decision. You're not an animal." So, for me, that works fine. I'm happier and healthier this way.

On the other hand, some single parents are not at all content with abstinence. For them, the difficulty is in finding a mate. Like Louise, a thirty-nine-year-old divorcée, they take a more traditional approach:

Being without a man is a big factor in my life. It's always there and I'm always aware of it. It hurts. It's both an innate and a conditioned need. There's something quite different about relating to a man and relating to a woman. I have lots of good women friends. We talk a lot about our emotions, share a lot. They support me a great deal but it's not the same as having a man who cares about me. It's not even so much the physical lovemaking. It's the reassurance that you are a worthwhile person, the sharing of good times, the discussing, the cooking and eating together.

Louise, looking for a deep relationship, may scare off a single father such as Simon, who is building a new life with his two-year-old son after six years of marriage:

Women anticipate maturity from you because you're a single father. It's a bit like you're schizophrenic: father versus lover. I'm not looking for a woman to fit into my life.

Women have neither less nor more need for sex than men. The need is particular to each human being. What is important, for both men and women, is to know what your own values are and to live by them—no matter what other people may say or think.

   Although some single parents are horrified at the thought, many turn to masturbation to relieve their sexual tension. According to a nurse who is the single mother of an eleven-year-old girl, masturbation has more than one benefit:

Apart from the pleasure and physical release obtained through masturbating, there is also the possibility of removing that air of sexual desperation you can see sometimes on the faces of the sexually hungry. In such cases, masturbation would be increasing the chances of meeting a suitable sex partner. A contented, relaxed look will not scare off a balanced personality, whereas despair may well attract the sexual exploiter.

Almost all single parents express conservative opinions about sexual activities. They have orthodox views on relating sex with love; they seem to wish to avoid any kind of promiscuity. And most seem to have a healthy attitude toward sex. One of the reasons for this could be the very latitude for sexual activity that single parents are free to enjoy.

Just the freedom to say yes or no is an enormously good feeling. None of this "wifely duty" bit. You choose who you want to have sex with and you don't have to account to anyone. All of your relationships, and the content of those relationships, are by choice, and that's great.

Sex is not necessarily the deepest form of communication between people. While it should be a two-way expression of sincere affection, it can also be a barrier to real communication. And many know that sex is frequently used as a weapon. So many taboos surround the subject—and so many pressures are brought to bear on our sex lives by myth and media—that it is a wonder that full enjoyment, as well as physical fulfillment, is ever achieved.

The sexually unhappy single parents are those who set impossibly high standards for their partners or themselves, or who wallow in self-despair about never finding the right kind of person. Sometimes there is an idea that everyone they meet is going to be like the partner who let them down or who did not work out. It is essential to get rid of this harmful notion and to realize that to seek perfection in another person—in whatever aspect, the sexual included—is foolish. Similarly, to assume that everyone else is like your previous partner, or will turn out to disappoint you in whatever way that person disappointed you, is dangerous.

A majority of single mothers say it is difficult to find "decent" men and that far too many of the men they come in contact with cannot see them as persons. They are seen only as sexual objects:

Ninety percent of the time, guys just want something physical. "Oh, you're separated, you have children, you're in need of a man." I guess they just want to warm your bed for a while.

Is it true that men are only interested in sex for its own sake, but women want more out of a relationship? No, although most of us believe this to be true. A man wants to be accepted and loved "for himself" just as much as a woman. Everyone has a need for recognition, warmth and acceptance: a need to be loved. Conversely, there are some women whose only apparent interest in a heterosexual relationship is sex.

Some single mothers react with near-puritanical attitudes because of society's implicit view of them as "fallen women." Such concepts take a long time to die, and the guilt feelings do not help, either. Just as the innocent rape victim wonders, "Did I do something to make this happen?", the single mother asks herself, "Am I giving out availability messages?" when she finds her friend's husband suddenly very solicitous of her (sexual) well-being. But he is responding as much to our stereotyped view of men—the he-man stud gallantly at the ready to satisfy the hapless damsel—as he is to any real sexual urge he may feel.

HOMOSEXUAL
SINGLE PARENTS

Some single parents are homosexual. Frequently such an adult acknowledges his or her gay tendencies only after years of marriage and parenthood. Barry, a homosexual and father of two boys, claims:

No one is completely heterosexual or completely homosexual. Yet it seems to be assumed that a gay father is going to involve his son in sexual acts. This is just as silly an assumption as that a girl visiting her straight father would be sexually molested. I think that's part of looking at gay people as if they are interested in persons of the same sex from only a sexual standpoint. Most gay people are not into having sex with young kids. Most cases involving child molesting are heterosexual, like 98 percent. There is an unwillingness to accept gay people as human beings.

Barry's own boys understand as much about the issue as six- and seven-year-olds can. They are proud of their father, whom they know as a warm, open person. (Barry is also well known publicly as a successful academic and as a social activist.) The boys said sometimes other children say unkind things, "but our dad's okay."

Single mothers may be less aware of their homosexual tendencies than are their male counterparts. "A lot of lesbians only become aware of their homosexuality in their thirties—and often following the breakup of a marriage," says Rhoda, a single mother of two children and a counselor of lesbians.

There is a large percentage of women who for years passively put up with the heterosexual role. They don't even realize for a while that anything is wrong, because they've been taught, as women, that they shouldn't be enjoying sex anyway.

LOCATE,
DATE, MATE

Less than 10 percent of a survey of British fathers who had lost their wives through death or desertion missed their wives sexually. Yet 24 percent missed their wives on sentimental and other occasions.

There may be several reasons for this, including the possibility that the single fathers are currently satisfying their sexual needs adequately. What is evident, however, is the continuing need for adult companionship.

Finding other adults to talk, let alone sleep, with is frequently difficult for single parents. Old friends, embarrassed by the grief over the death of the marriage partner, or reluctant to side with one or the other parent in a marriage dissolution, drop away. And nearly all single parents have faced the awkwardness of not being welcomed by friends who remain married. This is particularly felt when a marriage is threatened by the presence of a single parent happy with his or her lot.

Single fathers find that their male friends are unwilling to listen to their pain and perplexity. The friends will buy them a drink or introduce them to new women, but not let the single father talk. Discussing feelings is still considered unmanly by many men.

Where *do* single parents meet people of the opposite sex? In all the traditional places: workplace, evening courses, hobbies, sports, political parties, religious activities, dances and bars. Those who can afford it also try commercial dating services, although these are rarely satisfactory. Pursuing people is like hunting happiness: no matter your pace, you lose the race. Happiness hops farther out of reach the more you scramble after it. People jump out of the way of bulldozers, human or machine. This is why seeking "someone special" through commercial dating services or singles' socials is so frequently disappointing. Happiness is the by-product of meaning, which is found through love, work or creation. Similarly, friends or lovers appear when you need them, if your life has meaning. For most of us, a powerful impetus is the needs of, and love for, our children.

Organizations such as PWP and OPFA are great for socializing with adults and at least having contact with the opposite sex, although never-married single parents are likely to feel somewhat uncomfortable. They do not have the shared experience of a terminated marriage. They are also likely to be younger.

One way to meet people is to throw your own party. If you're short of cash, or even if you're not, ask each guest to bring food or drinks. Invite other singles and encourage them to bring others, including their former friends. So what if their relationship curdled? Milk that's sour to one person may be cream to another.

Or you could try a Bring-a-Buddy Brunch. Held on the same

principle as the party, but with less tension and formality, especially on a Sunday. It can be a relaxed way to meet new, interesting people, with none of the pressures of a formal date. Everyone can have a good time, even if your "someone special" doesn't appear this Sunday. With some forethought, you could include children. Older ones can help with refreshments, younger ones might entertain, or all could go off skating or whatever with one or two single parents. A Buddy Brunch can be a warm time for non-custody parents, too. Invite no fewer than six adults and no more than fifteen. Share the cleanup as well as the food. Brainstorm for themes (board games, Mexican eats or charades, for example), or leave it casual.

Perhaps, if you've tried all the above, you might try the newspaper "personals." But follow these safeguards: word your ad carefully, because your description of what you want in a man or woman says a lot about you, too. Always use a box number, because then you have a chance to weed out people who don't interest you. When you do follow up a reply, always arrange a meeting in a public place such as a restaurant and never reveal your full name, address or telephone number until you are sure you want to continue the relationship. Women can expect two to four dozen replies to a personal ad. Men may receive ten or twenty.

Single mothers looking for men should go where men congregate: the stock exchange, the race car track, handyman shows, the flying club or the local chess association, for instance. Single mothers who decide to train for a "male" occupation may discover romance along with their diplomas and tool kits. Certainly the numerical odds are greatly improved if you go where men predominate.

Single fathers, being outnumbered, do not face the same problem. There are often twenty women to one man in a single-parent organization, for instance.

The opposite sex is everywhere. There is no need to go through the complicated machinations that we often impose on ourselves. If you talk with people at the laundromat, the library, the supermarket or on the bus, you will probably find new friends. Most of us resent a transparent come-on; similarly, most of us appreciate an honest, especially shy or nervous, smile. Smiling is one of the best beacons we have to spread friendliness.

LEARNING
TO DATE AGAIN

If you've been out of the dating scene for years, plunging in can be terrifying. A single mother may be fearful at first about "picking up" men. (If it's any consolation, it's no easier for a man. After all, he is still expected to make the first move. A woman has only to smile and some male will probably speak to her.)

Some single parents, relearning to date, paradoxically will behave as though they are not interested. Why wonder why no one asks you out if you respond (for example, in a singles' bar) with a steely glare and a "I'm just here for the music" between clenched teeth?

"What do I say?" "What's expected these days? Instant sex?" "Do I tell my children?" Relax. There's an easy way to learn the steps to today's dating dance: ask a never-married single parent who's never dropped out, or a formerly married single parent who has recently dropped in.

Your own standards will tell you what to accept and what to reject. You may find, however, that what you thought was a firmly held belief fades fast. Lydia has been a one-man woman for twenty years. Married at eighteen, she had slept only with her husband, George. For months after the divorce, Lydia refused to date. Finally she accepted an invitation to dinner:

What an eye opener that was. I was barely in his apartment when he asked me if he could have dessert first. He meant me. Since then, I've dated many men who took it for granted that we'd have sex on the first date, but none of them were as crude about it as Sid. What surprised me more was how much I enjoyed it. Here I'd been putting myself down for even wanting sex, not to mention doing it with someone I wasn't in love with. But I bedded with anyone who wasn't totally revolting. And I loved it. All those guys wanted me. Me. And to think George said I was boring in bed. Well, let me tell you, I'm not boring now!

Earl, a forty-two-year-old single father, also found a new self-confidence through sleeping with a succession of casual partners:

It was so refreshing. No strings. No guilt. No games. Best of all, no impotence.

Both Lydia and Earl came from marriages in which they had felt sexually inadequate. Divorce was the final rejection. The life sentence pronounced by a dissatisfied spouse was shattered by impersonal sex: Lydia and Earl each received a much-needed feeling of being accepted.

Although some maintain the practice for years, most single parents who relish sex without commitment do so only for a short time. It is as though they are healed by the experience and go on, broadened and becalmed, to seek a more traditional relationship. You have to act in the way you feel is right. Casual sex is not for everyone. It may not really be for the person you've just asked to hop into bed (or who asked you). Perhaps that person, too, is struggling to decide what is permissible.

You have to face reality: you are single and you are entitled to live as a single. I don't think it's healthy to take a series of short-term flings. Don't hurt yourself. Be choosy. You've got the choice now.

If you go out with a friend of the same sex, do you expect the friend to pay? Why should a male be expected to pay for a female friend? If the relationship is a romantic one, should there be an expectation that the man will pay for the night out with dollars, and the woman with her body? Since women enjoy sex, too, we could just as illogically say the man has to pay twice: first with money and then with his body!

It's this kind of inequality that contented single parents are beyond. They are acutely conscious of the financial strains, the pressures of child care and the chores of home management. But, along with these restrictions is a paradoxical sense of personal freedom, of initiatives to be seized, of the excitement of life. Most are willing to share, to experience, to venture.

There are some single parents who find dating disastrous because they have not progressed out of their self-pity, a sure killer of any relationship. Nobody wants to listen to your troubles all the time. You must also be a listener. This will keep your mind off your own problems, and your friend will be relieved and impressed by being able to talk with an empathetic person.

When you meet another single parent, the exchange of information is frank and rapid: "You separated? How many kids? I'm divorced, got one boy. Do you work? Ex okay?" Previously married single parents often spot each other by the way we refer to our ex when speaking with the child (usually "your father" or "your mother") putting a verbal and psychological distance between ourself and our ex.

Single parents have an excellent opportunity to broaden their horizons through relationships of many kinds with persons of the opposite sex. This enjoyment can be maximized if intercourse is not always the prime objective in establishing new friendships:

Having men friends who are just that is one of the wonderful things about being a single mother.

FATAL
ATTRACTIONS

The more your self-awareness grows, the more likely it is that you can avoid falling into the common trap of becoming involved with yet another person like your ex. It is amazing how similar people can be beneath a surface dissimilarity, and how frequently a person will link up with just the kind of individual that is most destructive to him or her.

Why does your new partner—so different in looks, or occupation, or interests—turn out to be so similar to your ex? Because, like most single parents, you are a creature of habit: you seek essentially the same kind of person to respond to your needs. Probably you are not fully aware of those needs, but they form the die from which your behavior is cast. To recognize your behavior pattern is one step in learning to avoid unsatisfactory linkups. Another step is to decide what you really want in a mate.

Many of us are attracted by someone who has complementary characteristics to ourselves. Thus a weak person feels drawn to a strong person, a homebody to a partygoer, a sex enthusiast to a prude. Others tend to couple with someone whose characteristics, far from complementing their own, are so similar as to provoke competition. A musically creative person, for example, might be bewitched by someone who is artistically creative; an ambitious architect starry-eyed over an ardent journalist; a workaholic bowled over by a sportsaholic.

NON-FIT PATTERNS

Whether you are the kind of person generally attracted to a complementor or a competitor, trouble arises when the pattern no longer fits. Just as you can't cut a dress from a pattern designed for a coat, your complementary relationship founders when one of you no longer complements the other. Similarly, a competitive relationship founders when one partner drops out or, conversely, gains too much. All Amy's and Bob's friends thought they were a perfect (complementary) match.

I guess you could call me a dependent type. I clung to Bob like he was a life raft and I was a nonswimmer in the middle of the Atlantic. But the irony was that after ten years of marriage I had changed—I was much more independent, took courses, got a job outside the house—he couldn't stand my being me. He was so used to being Mr. Strong he just couldn't adjust to being Mr. Equal. I see that now, but I had to go through the same kind of thing with Andrew and Clive before I realized I was repeating this role of weak, dependent me leaning on a man and then growing independent of him.

In contrast, Sheila and Tony were competitors from the beginning. Tony wrote:

We met at a professional swim meet. Sheila was very, very good. So was I. But I got the edge on her when she lost several years through pregnancy and raising the kids. It was too much for her—losing out on her professional status to me, I mean. Now I've got the kids and she's a swim-team coach. Do you think I learned from that? Nope. My next girl friend was a tennis champ. Our affair lasted six months. I couldn't live with all the publicity and awards she was getting.

UNHEALTHY PATTERNS

A person is not Mr. or Ms Wrong in isolation, but in a particular mix of emotions and behavior with you. What *you* do and feel is at least half of why someone is wrong for you. Often the pattern is unhealthy from the start. A complementary relationship may be one where one partner abuses the other. A competitive relationship may be one in which the partners are continually jealous and bickering.

Why would a single parent who has escaped from one unhealthy complementary or competitive relationship walk straight into another? Studies of battered wives yield a clue: such women were often battered children. In other words, their pattern was established early: they learned to see themselves as worthless, as deserving only of being beaten. Their emotional radar tunes in accurately and automatically to a man who will continue the abuse.

Less extreme, but still serious if you are the victim, is the knack of teaming up with someone who ignores you. You may even be drawn to the person by the very thing that is going to leave you in the cold: like Todd, a single father of three, who so admired his friend Cheryl's dedication to her career. Later, her obsession with work excluded Todd (and the children) almost completely from her life. When Todd met Anna, he thought for sure *she* was Ms Right. Anna was no career woman. In fact, her enthusiasm centered on gardening as a hobby. She built her own greenhouse so she could garden all year round. Once again, Todd took second place. His pattern was to seek out obsessed women, so wrapped up in work or hobby (or charity or politics) that he would always be ignored. It is almost as though Todd needs confirmation that he is unimportant. Maybe he learned this from his mother and sisters. The sisters were several years older than Todd and frequently out of town with their mother on singing engagements. Todd would have been in the way and there never seemed to be any time left over for the women to be with him.

DENIAL PATTERNS

Some single parents, like Lana, a thirty-seven-year-old never-married mother, fail to see how their own behavior brings them exactly the kind of man they don't want. Lana complains that she meets only macho men who bore her with their "tough" act. Yet Alan, a gentle person who has dated Lana, says she provokes him into "tough-guy" actions by making fun of anything he says that is the least bit tender.

Another denial pattern is that of the person who claims to be miserable because each partner turns out to be immature, alcoholic, emotionally crippled or otherwise in need of being cared for. Perhaps a need to nurture is at the root of this continual search for someone to look after; perhaps the need is to find someone to feel superior toward. The relationship dies because the caring person refuses to admit to his or her satisfaction in the role.

RELATIONSHIP
EXERCISE

Here is an exercise designed to help you out of the rut. Fill in and analyze the three Relationship Charts. Discover whether yours is a Non-fit, an Unhealthy or a Denial pattern. Or perhaps some of each. Read over your comments. Do you see a pattern in your behavior?

SLEEP-OVER
DATES

Some single parents worry about whether they should sleep with sexual partners while the children are in the house.

It could be very awkward. When my child was young it was not such a problem, although I was nervous at every sound. I wouldn't recommend it. I did choose for a while to live with someone and I had to cope with a very upset ten-year-old daughter.

It was necessary to explain that I was choosing a lifestyle for my own reasons, that I needed an adult male because I am an adult female. These were facts of life that she might not understand at present but would someday. She adjusted and finally accepted the situation.

Many separated and divorced mothers hesitate to have intercourse in their homes because they fear legal action by their former partners to label them as unfit mothers. In the middle of her divorce case, one woman said:

I have detectives following me. My phone is tapped. How do you handle your sexual needs? It is a need like eating, drinking and sleeping. In my particular case, I said to hell with the detectives and to hell with the telephone tapping. I'm going to listen to myself. I'm not going to go against my own moral judgments—I don't believe a man should be brought into the house and I don't believe you should have intercourse in your home if there are young children who might wake during the night. But for your own sanity, you've got to have that release.

If you can afford to go out of town, great, but if you can't, then any other arrangement that suits your own moral judgment is fine. I don't think you change your moral values just because you're single.

If you are nervous or ashamed about your sexual partners—or your lack of them—then your child will likely be nervous, too. On the other hand, what you are natural about, the child will generally accept, though not always in the way you might expect:

One morning, after I had stayed overnight in a friend's bed (she's a single mother with an adorable five-year-old girl), her daughter came into the

RELATIONSHIP
CHART

MY IDEAL MATE WOULD HAVE THE FOLLOWING CHARACTERISTICS:	I PICKED THIS CHARACTERISTIC BECAUSE . . .

RELATIONSHIP
CHART

WHAT I LIKE(D) ABOUT MY EX(ES)*:	WHAT I DISLIKE(D) ABOUT MY EX(ES):

* Start with your latest and then go back to the ex before last, and so on, as far back as you wish to go.

RELATIONSHIP
CHART

HOW DID I BEHAVE AROUND MY EX(ES)*? (MEEK? AGREEABLE? CARING? DOMINEERING?)
THE PATTERN I SEE IS . . .

* For example, "With ex number 3 I was . . . , with ex number 2 I was . . . ."

bedroom where my friend was dressing. In horrified tones, the little girl said, "Did you get dressed in front of *him*?"

Sometimes openness leads to the kind of dilemma Kate found herself in:

Both my daughters are teen-agers and outspoken. They know I have a sex life. But they want to tell me who I should see and not see. I'll listen to them, but I made it clear *I'm* the one who decides who I'll date. Anyway, it came to a head when Helmut, an old friend, invited me for a holiday in Holland. Rosalind, my eldest, came with me. We stayed in a hotel and it didn't bother Rosalind a bit that Helmut and I were sharing a room.

But when we came back Janet, who was thirteen at the time, found out (from my ex) and she was frightfully upset. I explained to Janet that I was old enough to know what I was doing and that Helmut and I were very fond of each other. I guess it's going to take a while for her to really understand.

When the children are not only adolescents, but also of the opposite sex to their parent, it is not uncommon for them to react like this single mother's sons when she became involved with a man after four dateless years:

The boys are very concerned. They put me on a pedestal. They see me leading a relatively celibate life and they've heard me complain about being alone, and all of a sudden someone comes into my life and I feel that they really resent it. They had mixed feelings about this person staying all night.

I had always told them that they should only be sexually involved with someone they cared deeply about, and I wasn't even living that philosophy. I wasn't deeply involved with this person but I was enjoying him and I needed his company; it was good for me emotionally and psychologically. The boys were beautiful. They said, "Well, that's all right mum. If it makes you happy that's the most important thing."

But it was a very short-term relationship. I don't know how they would react to a long-term one.

My feeling is that with teen-age sons, they come first. They're my priority and, as far as my own life, my sex life, that's going to have to come after they leave me. Unless the person who means a lot in my life is going to be very, very congenial and very much able to relate to my sons in a positive, healthy, meaningful way. And I don't think that's an easy thing for most men to do with teen-age boys.

Some single parents feel that intercourse in the home is fine if you have an ongoing, deep relationship with the other adult. A lot depends on the age of your child.

WHAT TO TELL
YOUR CHILD

Your child will not be well served if you never go out for fear of arousing anxiety in him. It can be hard on you to go out on the town while little Fred is pleading and screaming for you to stay. But you will find that after a time—and given a warm interaction between you and Fred—your consistent reappearance will be sufficient reassurance to Fred that you are not going away forever.

How soon you begin dating after a marital breakup or death of your spouse depends partly on your child's readiness. Does he or she find your constant attention overpowering? If so, your child may be relieved that some of your concern is going to be diverted. This is the view of some teen-age girls tired of worrying about their single mothers: "Get out as much as possible to meet new people—then we don't feel the responsibility for your social life." Or, in the wistful words of fifteen-year-old Gordon, "I wish my mum would date someone. That's what she needs, a man. I think she'd be happier."

On the other hand, your child may be used to having you all to herself. If this is the reality you've provided, you'll have to proceed cautiously. Explain in words and actions that you need adult friends, but this won't change your love for her.

If you don't believe in an exclusive relationship—or if you are heady with the excitement of sharing your bed with several successive partners—you may be faced with the same dilemma as Eileen:

A single mother may want to have many lovers. How can she help the child cope with this? Especially when the kid might think, "If a boyfriend can't depend on mum, then how can I?"

Some single parents reassure the child that numerous lovers do not mean a lessening of their love for the child. This is how one divorcée explained to her daughter:

Look, my commitment to you is forever. You'll always be my daughter. I'll always love you. Nothing and no one can come between us. What I do with my friends, though, is my business. Do you feel you don't have enough time with me because I'm out so often? That's another issue. It would be just as wrong as if I missed time with you because I was always studying or watching television or going alone to fashion shows. Our time together is precious.

It is surely better for your child to grow up seeing you affectionate and interacting with other people than to gain the impression that you exist in an asexual vacuum. But don't be surprised if your child imitates your dating behavior.

Single parents who want to date face practical problems. Someone has to look after your child if he is young. This is one reason that it is good to get to know other single parents in your neighborhood. If you get along, you can take turns baby-sitting. That way everyone benefits: you save money and guilt feelings and the children have others to play with while you are out. You can also bring the date back to your own home when it's your turn for a free night.

HOW YOUR CHILD
RATES YOUR DATES

Your child is very much involved and affected by your dating. You must be prepared to answer questions. A few single parents, like Darlene, share everything:

I tell my children everything about sex. It's normal, it's all around and it's great—at the right time and with the right person.

But more of us feel like Vivian, who says:

While I think it is important to be open with children I also think it important not to have to explain everything—I personally am rather private about *my* sex life although I am open on the subject in general terms.

Some single parents allow their child to veto dates. Many teenagers say they "like being consulted by mum about her dates." You may want to chat with your child about his opinion of your dates. But to give the child veto power is to surrender your responsibility as an adult. And to place too weighty a burden on your child.

The child may make rude remarks to the date if he feels you are deserting him. At the other extreme, he may make overly warm overtures to a date that he takes a fancy to. In each case, the child has to be taught to behave politely but not falsely. One of your child's preoccupations may be, "Are you going to marry so-and-so?" A child may ask if you're sleeping with the date. How you answer will depend on how clear you are about your attitudes and how much you feel is appropriate to share with your child. Margo, on her own with a daughter for five years, was not telling all to her daughter. Nevertheless, she understood that what thirteen-year-old Claudia wanted was reassurance that Margo would not neglect her for a man:

Claudia has been very curious about a male friend of mine. She assumed, I think, that male plus female makes sex. While it often does, I pointed out that this was not necessarily so. (In fact, this friend is homosexual.) I told her this and I also told her that if there was anything she needed to know (e.g., whether I'm planning on living with someone), I would certainly discuss it with her. I think this helped her to accept other male friends more comfortably.

Claudia and her friends want their single mothers to have a sex life ("It makes for a happier person," they said), but, "Please keep it off the premises because we don't want a stranger coming in to take the role of father."

It is not easy for an adolescent to handle her own feelings of sexuality, let alone her mother's. Perhaps the daughter is embarrassed by knowledge of her mother's sexual activity (especially if, prior to becoming a single parent the mother was a spouse in a traditional marriage). Perhaps, also, to the child, her mother sleeping with a date is symbolic of ultimate disloyalty to her father.

Simply keeping sex out of the home, however, doesn't necessarily resolve the dilemma. Connie, deserted at twenty-seven, felt she needed sex and male companionship after her husband walked out, but

I really could not explain my right to certain fulfillments to a five-year-old daughter and two-year-old son. Neither did I have any wish to be questioned about what I considered normal needs.

A year passed before I began to date, although I did have parties, dinners, picnics, and so forth that included male friends and the children. I had decided bars and discos or single's things were not for me. I did manage to meet men mostly through friends, but my first relationship did

not begin till after a year. It lasted one and a half years and then deterio-
rated badly for a year.

I sort of tried to keep the children part of the new set-up. I was home a
lot and I did not have my boyfriend sleep over. I felt very strongly that,
unless I cared enough to make a stand about my morals or have my children exposed to bedroom scenes or morning competitions for "bathroom
and breakfast," I'd maintain or rather try to maintain some sort of nor-
malcy in their lives. The pressures were tough and probably in some way
contributed to the dissolution of the relationship.

If there is one thing a child feels strongly, it is that your date has no
business telling her how to live. One of the surest ways to antago-
nize your child is to allow the date to criticize the way the child
dresses, talks, walks, eats or whatever. This is not to say your date
should be indifferent to your child, but that such criticism should be
discussed privately, between you and the date. In any case, it is
unwise to date someone who resents your child, because you will be
torn between them. And because it's extremely unlikely such a
person will stick around for long. As Rita puts it:

I realized we were a package deal and anyone entering or venturing into
our world had to accept the reality of it.

One of the indicators of progress in single parenthood is that today
it is out of date to tell your child a date is "Uncle" or "Cousin" or
"Aunty" so-and-so. It is doubtful that children were ever deceived
by such euphemisms.

Your dates are your friends. Whether or not the relationship is
sexual, your child wants and needs to meet your friends because, as
one adolescent put it, "We need adults, too."

Your child may grow fond of one of your dates. If your relationship with that friend crumbles, the breakup will be easier for
your child to handle if you've had ongoing, nonsexual relationships
with other adults. The child will see that not all adult friendships are
doomed to be short-lived; not everyone he likes or loves is bound to
vanish. If you have the maturity to continue being a friend when
your date is no longer a mate, your child's relationship with your
ex-lover can continue. Or, at least, wind down gradually. If the
breakup is unavoidably abrupt, then you must face the loss and the
hurt with your child. Share your grief. Encourage the child to say
what he feels. Don't be melodramatic. If you are separated or di-

vorced, follow similar guidelines to those outlined for explaining your initial entrance into single parenthood. Emphasize that the former friend has not broken with you on account of the child, but because of differences between the two of you (or because of a transfer out of town, or you are no longer in love or whatever the reason). Kaisu found such a breakup was

once again a time for inner delving, and after a period of great guilt and many honest confrontations with myself and the children, I emerged again, whole—different, but whole—and the children were strong enough to be a comfort, still be open about people and optimistic about the future.

EIGHT

CHILDREN: EXTRA SPECIAL PEOPLE

TO CHOOSE SINGLE PARENTHOOD is to make a commitment to a child, a commitment that rewards us a thousandfold. A child is an inspiration: when we're feeling down, just seeing her can perk us up. A child is a comfort: his trust in us makes us glow. A child provides purpose: we have a motive for living. A child is an honor: for a short while, we are graced by her presence. A child is precious: a privilege to know. But most of all, a child is love. And the reason we enjoy being single parents. Rita sums up how most of us feel:

I'd like my children to be strong, independent, have a pride in themselves and be caring, loving adults. I'd like to give them the spring blossoms, waves breaking along a shore, the smell of the forest. I'd like to give them the world—but really the ability to just see the beauty and joy of it all and I know I can't give them that. I can only be me for them.

HELP YOUR CHILD CONQUER GUILT AND ANXIETY

Children who lose a parent through death will be anxious about the possible death of the remaining parent. They must be helped through their grieving, and reassured about the health of the survivor. The child's reaction will depend largely on the adults around him. If they encourage him to talk about his feelings, to remember the good times he had with the parent when alive, then the child will be able to accept the loss and live normally. One widow found her children were a tremendous comfort to her after her husband died. She shared her grief with them; for a while they all slept together because the youngsters were so scared that she might die, too.

Another widow found that frank talk helped both her and her daughter:

I was determined not to wipe out the happiness we had while my husband was alive. He made us a family. And we're still a family. I want Maria to remember how wonderful he was and not just brood over the loss.

Frankness, sharing and keeping to a familiar routine all help the child survive the numbness, confusion and anxiety that occur after a parent dies.

The child of a never-married parent may have a different anxiety: "Will I grow up to be like the parent I don't know?" To avoid letting the child build possibly harmful fantasies, let her know as much as possible about the absent parent and arrange for them to meet. When the child is old enough, if she wishes she can develop her own relationship.

A child from a divorced or separated family, no matter how innocent, is likely to feel guilt over the split between his parents. He may not say anything but may change drastically, becoming quiet and withdrawn from previously being boisterous and outgoing. Soon after Desmond's wife walked out after eleven years of marriage, he remarked:

It's difficult to say how the kids have reacted. I was in a state. They tried to protect me, pretending it didn't happen. They knew something was wrong and somehow they didn't want to talk about it. They had a burden: not knowing what might hurt me, what to say and so on. They became very cautious and quiet.

A child probably will react, not only with feelings of guilt ("What did I do to make mummy and daddy break up?"), but also with self-recrimination ("I must be bad, otherwise why did mummy/daddy go away?"). How should this burden on your child be handled? First, you have to accept that the adult *you* no longer live with is still extremely important to the child.

I was torn into emotional shreds when my daughter sobbed herself to sleep because she missed her father so much, especially since I would rather never see him again.

You must control your outbursts of grievances against your ex, no

matter how rotten you believe the ex-partner to be. Unlike the Toronto single father who didn't seem to care who heard him:

Half the people on the streetcar could hear the loud, bitter complaining of
the man whose little son cowered in fear and embarassment.

"Why weren't you ready when I came?" asked the man belligerently.
"Did you have a wash for a change?" he continued. "Why weren't you
ready? I've told you before I want you ready at one sharp."

The man went on and on. He paid no real attention to the child who was
scrunching lower and lower in the seat.

"What did you do last week?" the man persisted. "Go somewhere in one
of your mother's fancy boyfriends' cars? She knows I can't afford a damn
car. Did you wash? Why don't you smarten up? She's not too bright if she
thinks she can treat me like this. You're supposed to be ready when I come.
On the dot . . . ."

This went on for twenty minutes. The father—pouring out his hurt
and misery—seemed unaware of the effect his outburst was having
on his son. Would it be surprising if the little boy returned to his
mother overwhelmed with confused feelings of guilt, shame and
anger? That she be faced with an unruly son who tests her love by
boisterous behavior (or conversely, by timid withdrawal)? How
should she react? She may be indifferent, and thus add to the boy's
sorrow. More likely she would know that she should be patient,
comforting and accepting of her son . . . and not say the nasty
things she's thinking about the brute she used to be married to. Yet
her own hurt at seeing her son miserable might well awaken her
guilt—in turn causing her to lash out angrily at the boy.

There is a middle way between an unrealistic head-over-heart
cool control and a surrendering to the passions of the moment. This
is how Marcia, thirty-five and separated for six months, handled a
similar situation:

I cuddled my son. I started to tell him I knew he felt bad and that he hadn't
done anything wrong but I began crying and couldn't stop for what
seemed like ages. He looked even more upset. So I said, "Look, I'm feeling
lousy too. Part of it is that I'm angry at your father for talking the way he
does. Part of it is that I feel responsible—like it's my fault. But it's not you
or me or your father. It's all of us. You know, there's a song called 'You
Always Hurt the One You Love.' Your father and I both love you very
much. But sometimes when we want to tell you, it all comes out mixed up
and we end up being nasty. Daddy says things to you that he really wants

to throw at me. Sometimes I get so mad at him I feel like screaming, but I pick on you instead. That's not right and I'm sorry. It's not your fault at all. I feel a bit calmer now. Why don't you talk about how you feel?"

Marcia's son talked out the pain caused by his father's outbursts, and Marcia did her best to listen impartially.

Many single parents have to learn to speak honestly, but not destructively, to their children about their relationship with the other parent. No good purpose is served by downgrading a child's father or mother directly to the child. You, as a single mother or father, might explain to your child that although you and your ex no longer wish to be together, you both love her. It is essential to let the child know that the separation was not caused by her, and to accept her tears and hurt.

I told my daughter not to keep her tears in. I would sit and cuddle her and she would sob for a while, talk about her mother. There was no way a six-year-old could understand the reasons for our separation, but she could, and did, understand that I loved and accepted her, that it was okay to cry on my shoulder for her mother.

Many single parents have discovered that to help their children, first they had to overcome their own feelings of bitterness and guilt:

Before I decided to divorce my husband, I had gone over, in my head, all the guilts. After I had made my decision, I felt quite at ease with my situation. The children were young, but I explained the situation to them and through the years have elaborated. Their father and I were just not suited to each other—we didn't hate each other—it was an adult thing entirely separate from our love for them.

Sometimes the child's emotions will erupt in outbursts of anger. Then—just as for adults—it's a good idea to have a special punching pillow, a drawer of smashable things or even a rolled-up newspaper that the angry child can beat against a wall.

The youngster's anxiety is best coped with by your being physically present, if at all possible, until the child settles down. The child needs lots of affection, cuddling and playing. But ease up as soon as she shows signs of being ready to face the world again. No child ever suffered from a surfeit of love and affection, but many have died inwardly by being smothered with overprotection.

Your child might also benefit from discussion with a group of children in similar circumstances. Such groups—like the one in Hennepin County, Minnesota—are part of the court services, while others can be found in community organizations.

OPEN UP
TO YOUR CHILD

Some single parents discuss everything with their children, but the pain of your disputes with your ex may be too heavy for a child. Few of us are able to argue calmly or rationally, especially in the early stages of single parenthood arising from separation or divorce. Heated outbursts serve only to further bewilder the hurt child. When the issue intimately concerns the child, however, then he should be included in the discussion. Such issues as which parent the child should live with and which school to attend are the type of disputes to be settled with the child. To avoid an adversary situation in which the child is forced to crown a winner, it is wise to have an impartial adult arbitrate: a common friend or a counselor, preferably someone chosen by the child.

In the long run, most single parents, divorced or not, will find themselves agreeing with Fiona, whose children are now thirteen, fifteen and eighteen:

Since the divorce six years ago, I think my children have become more mature and more independent. There just hasn't been time to baby them. I talk with them about things a woman usually only discusses with her husband. But by telling each other about our feelings, I think they've become more sensitive emotionally. They understand human emotions better. This means they have an easier time getting along with adults.

And many single parents find, like Simon, a twenty-nine-year-old single father, that,

alone, it's easier to be honest with my son. I also learned that Ronny had to be able to say to me whatever he felt about the separation . . . whatever he felt, without me contradicting him.

THE ONLY
CHILD

Some single parents of only children are concerned that their children may grow up too self-centered. No evidence exists of a correlation between being an only child and being selfish. But if the parent feels this may happen, there are various steps that can be taken. Apart from day-care and school experiences, the child could have friends visit overnight. Or the parent might consider having another child by birth, adoption or fostering. Two children of roughly the same age are generally easier to look after than children of different ages.

Another fear is the danger of too intense a relationship between parent and child. The intensity of the relationship is set by the parent. Fear of its being too intense should prod the parent to take positive actions: to get out more, to make new friends, to mix with other families. A never-married mother with one son says, "The best advice I ever got was not to live in isolation but to share my son with other people."

One child alone can develop a healthy sense of self-worth and security through the close relationship with her parent, something that a child in competition with siblings might not gain so readily.

ENCOURAGE YOUR CHILD
TO BE INDEPENDENT

Children in single-parent families are noticeably more responsible, self-reliant and mature than children of comparable ages from coupled-parent families. This comes about partly from what is usually a necessity: helping around the house and having to look after themselves. Susan is one example. The twenty-five-year-old daughter of a single woman, also from a single-parent family, she writes:

In our case, my father died in 1962. My youngest sister was three and my oldest brother seventeen. There were seven of us, three boys and four girls. We were brought up and worked on our own farm. We were brought up to like school and people, work, go to church, and not be spoiled with money. We had a country school of thirty pupils then and had to go to high school in our town later.

We had to work to get anything we wanted, which gave us something to look forward to. Mum got $65 a month and our rather small family allowance, which went mainly on bills and a few things for the house. My mother didn't care to get married again and she hasn't got the best education. Her father died, too, when they were kids. I think we were brought up as normal as anyone else. Most of our neighbors were farmers and maybe some didn't get along as well as us (maybe, in many cases, it is best to have only one parent).

Throughout childhood there are specific signs of independence, from crossing streets alone to dating and driving. You have to judge when your child is ready for each step. Some parents ignore the child and force independence too soon. Others coddle the child, not allowing him to act appropriately for his age. Listen to your child. Question whether it is your own fear, rather than the child's unreadiness, which prompts you to hold her back. The more children learn, by example and instruction, to look after themselves, in all aspects of life, the better prepared they are to become capable adults. At the same time, an emotional burden is lifted from you. The sooner a child dresses herself the sooner the responsibility is lifted from you. It is a step toward self-reliance.

Most children, even preschoolers, can learn to keep their room or area tidy. A four-year-old can set a table and make his bed. There is a line to draw between making your child a drudge and helping him develop respect for his and your home. Children also learn by example. When Bill's son saw that his five-year-old cousin ran her own bath, he soon learned to do it, too.

The three youngsters of Mical, a seamstress suddenly widowed at thirty-four, are learning the value of money:

They each receive an allowance, which goes up according to age and responsibility. They are supposed to buy certain basics such as pens and pencils, hair ribbons. And they are supposed to contribute to birthdays. Then they have other things for which they get extra. Cleaning cat boxes is worth 30¢ and the one who cleans the dog mess outside gets 25¢. And they all help in the house. That's basic, but on the other hand, if they do extra they get something for that.

Many single parents feel strongly that a child should *not* be paid for helping around the house. If you pay an adult, it is because for him or her it is a job, providing necessary income. But to pay your child might make him think he shouldn't do anything in the house unless he receives a cash benefit. As one single father with five sons says:

Children ought to be part of the home they live in, dirty in, play in, sleep in. It's their home, too, and they are responsible for chores, each according to his ability. It's also thoughtful and considerate. It's a great leveling agent. It's a good learning experience (and a necessary evil). It's a fact of life and everybody has to cooperate or things just don't work.

Fifteen-year-old Sharon agrees and adds emphatically: *"Don't do all the housework yourself and then lay a guilt trip on your kid."* A single mother who adopted two girls forty years ago adds:

Children should work around the house; they should not be paid for this. They are part of the family. You do things for them and they should do things for you. In that way they learn to be a family, and that you do things for each other and that they should do thoughtful acts.

Such preparation pays off when you are sick:

When I'm ill, we just manage as best we can. Usually friends step in. I've always made the children help a great deal in the house. I think it's necessary. And I think it's good for them as well. So they are all learning to cook. In this way it is much easier when I am sick because they more or less know what has to be done about tidying up and cleaning the house.

Work outside the home should be relative to a child's age and abilities. The money earned should be hers. You have an excellent opportunity to introduce your child to saving and budgeting. Guide her choice of purchases, but don't take her money. She earned it and should be able to make her own mistakes. Penelope has for two years been raising her three children on her salary as a nurse, plus,

I get an alimentary allowance for the children from their father—that is for the necessities. Allowances for the children are a luxury that right now is rather difficult. The children understand the problems and are encouraged to be economical. They have, in the past, argued that their father gives money for them and they ought to have some control. Instant veto. They get an allowance according to their needs for transportation, school supplies and occasionally, for treats.

Single parents often report that their older children, who are aware of the tricky state of home finances, will spontaneously offer some of their earnings to help out. Any manner in which your child is being useful, housework or money or something else, adds immeasurably to her self-image—if appreciated by you.

QUALITY TIME
WITH YOUR CHILD

One way to show appreciation of your child is to spend quality time
with him. Many single parents, particularly those who work outside the home, bemoan the shortness of time they have, not only for
themselves but for their children. Quality time is the answer to both
dilemmas.

Quality time is the time you spend being *with* your child, not
merely in the physical proximity. Quality time is when you share
yourself with your child. The activities can be simple: helping with
homework, going for a walk, talking over something that is important to her, reading together, playing games, gardening. Or the
activity may be more complex. It's not the what that counts, it's the
who. You interact with your child as the unique person that she is.
In so doing, not only does your child learn and enjoy, but you feel
the main pleasure of parenthood. Quality time is well defined by a
twenty-three-year-old busy mother of three:

You could spend your whole day with your child and the child not be fulfilled. But you can spend an hour, and he'll keep that, it will mean more to
him that you spent one full hour with him alone than just a few minutes
throughout the day.

A single father who is a university professor restricts 5:30 to 8:00
P.M. solely for his son. Those two and a half hours are sacred. He
will not make any appointment or other commitment that would
intrude on his son's time.

I've organized my life so I take him to school in the morning and pick him
up at 5:30. From then till 8:00 I don't answer the phone. Weekends are his,
too. Maybe there is a danger of overprotection. It's going to have to sort
itself out. It's a day-by-day learning experience.

Una, a waitress with two preteens, has a slightly different attitude:

Time seems rather irrelevant. Often I'm rushed and very busy, at other
times I'm relaxed and easy. I like my kids (not only love them); they're
O.K. Evenings are pretty much their time. If I'm busy, then they have to
wait—unless they asked for my attention first. When I'm with them, I'm
very much with them and I've decided not to feel guilty about the number
of hours.

Some single parents—ones who delight in increased closeness to their children—say that even fifteen minutes a day quality time is enough. Arnold says his eight-year-old daughter "is much easier to handle because she knows that if I'm too busy right now to talk with her she'll at least have my undivided attention for fifteen minutes at eight o'clock." Arnold notes that few children ever get real attention so this minimum concentrated time, although short, is really appreciated. "The child experiences how important she is to you, providing you concentrate on what she wants during your time together." The minimum quality time often extends into longer periods. The idea is particularly useful when there are several children. Each gets a special time of every day that belongs just to him or her—and the parent.

TWO PARENTS, ONE AT A TIME

Naturally, a child who has but one parent will cling tenaciously. That is understandable. But you must guard against three things. The first is gripping the child too closely, because of your own needs. The second is using the child as a substitute spouse. (Your son is not "the man of the house" now that his father is gone. The boy is your son, not a replacement husband. Similarly, a girl in a one-parent family should never be regarded as a "little mother.") The third is putting the child in the position of being torn between his loyalties and love for each parent.

Far too much is heard about children being used as pawns between bickering parents. The analogy is inaccurate; but the intent is clear. Parents caught in this destructive pattern must take a good look at themselves and make a conscientious effort not to continue tearing the child apart. Never say to the child as an insult, "You're just like your father," advises one divorced mother.

Another aspect of this tug-of-war bothers Katrina, a recently impoverished single mother:

If my three daughters spend a month with their father, he'll be jetting them to Greece, to Miami, all over. How can I explain living in a two-room apartment to them after they experience all the goodies he'll shower on them once a year?

Katrina is making a mistake common to many single parents in this

child-sharing situation. (Though the extremes of wealth and property probably would not be as far apart as in her case.) Worried
about having to exist on far less income than her ex, she thinks the
children will rebel against living with her in relative poverty. But
children are not fools. And they are usually much closer to their
feelings than adults are. While they may enjoy material goodies, it
is the bond of caring that really matters to them. Children sense the
difference. A shower of gifts is no substitute for love.

If both parents love the child, then the one who has her most of
the time should see the days the child spends with the other parent
as a wonderful thing. The child's regular absence is an opportunity
that many sole custody single parents would envy. After all, shuttle
parents have all the joys of family life part of the time and all the
joys of bachelor life the rest of the time.

JOINT
CUSTODY

Single parents are choosing joint custody not just because it offers
them the best of both family and bachelor life, but because it spares
the child a potentially ugly battle in court. Quite a few women
choose joint custody to avoid the stigma of being labeled "an un-
caring mother": even in instances where a father is more inclined to
the parental role, society can be harsh in its judgment of the "aban-
doning" mother.

Joint-custody agreements share the joys and responsibilities of
child caring between parents. Each parent has equal legal responsibility for the child. The child spends half the time in one parent's
home and half in the other's. This involves splitting weeks, months
or even years. Sometimes the child stays put and the parents take
turns living with her. Joint custody demands strong commitment
by each parent—plus an open dialogue so one parent isn't burdened
full-time and the other doesn't become a Sunday Santa.

Yet old ways of doing things take a long time to die. One skep-
tical lawyer protests:

Joint custody introduces an additional element of instability. The child
never knows if he's coming or going. He builds up friendships in one area,
but can't sustain them because he's continually going to the other parent's
home.

A single father—who, though his ex has legal custody, has worked out an unofficial joint custody arrangement—replies:

How can it be wrong for the child to keep both parents? For each of us to still be fully involved with our daughter, and yet have free time, too? That instability argument doesn't make much sense. I used to see my daughter every weekend so she was shunting back and forth anyway. The difference now is that we have enough time to be natural with each other. Cheryl has friends in both neighborhoods. Is that bad?

Not all single parents are able to work out satisfactory joint-custody agreements. But the reason is not mutual hostility and anger. Some ex-spouses who hate each other still manage to agree upon the details of joint custody. These are the ones who can sort out the marital issues from the parental issues. Their mutual love for the child overrides personal animosity. There must, though, be sufficient belief in the other parent's competence as a parent. The actual joint-custody agreement (which goes beyond mere physical custody) may be more easily worked out with the aid of an impartial adult. Impartial, that is, toward the parents. Partiality of the friend, counselor, cleric or court worker toward the child would be fine. A teen-ager will, of course, want to have a direct say in the arrangements.

Here are the kinds of points that have to be settled between parents trying to arrange joint custody:

- How many stable elements can we build into our child's new life? (Will she stay in the same school, same neighborhood?)
- Will we each make a commitment to stay in the same town?
- What's the best plan for the time to be spent by our child with each of us? (Half of each week? Alternate every six months? Every year?)
- Have we considered the child's feelings? (And explained how this way everyone wins, and the child doesn't lose either parent?)
- Will we share equally the costs of the child's medical care, clothes, education, camp? Or does one of us feel able to contribute more financially? Should we have a joint account for the child's expenses? Or should each of us be responsible only for expenses that arise when the child is with us?
- Will we meet from time to time to discuss our child's development and changes to the custody agreement? Will we need a third party to help?

• What will be best for our child at vacation times?
• Do we need neutral drop-off points to avoid unnecessary encounters?

Clearly, the details of a joint-custody agreement will differ from family to family. One arrangement has three children alternating every three and a half days between their parents' Manhattan apartments since 1971. The children are thriving despite (or because of) the vastly different life-styles of their mother and father. Mother is strict and vegetarian. Father is casual and a meat-eater. Another joint-custody arrangement in New York has the daughter alternate every six months between her mother's East Side apartment and her father's West Side flat. Her parents are good friends who meet frequently. They attend school plays and parent-teacher meetings together and each maintains a typical teen-age room for the daughter. Friends and rules of behavior are the same no matter which room is home.

THE SHUTTLE PARENT

There are things to be learned from joint-custody bargaining that can be useful to the single parent who has a more traditional child-custody arrangement, which often involves having the child during the week while the other parent has the child weekends.

You might tactfully mention the following suggestions to your ex (or buy him or her a copy of this book). There are few rules that apply to all, but most single parents in the child-shuttling situation agree on the following:

• Shuttle parents have to make a special effort to involve the child in their normal life. A wild round of commercial entertaining is no substitute for simply being with the child. Far better to spend the time doing natural, ordinary things, such as cooking together. The ordinary becomes extraordinary because you are not trying to buy affection with movies, candies and time killers.
• Both parents have to bury their differences long enough to make the most satisfactory arrangements about pick-up and return of the child, weekend activities, homework, etc. Arrange the schedule as soon as the two of you can, preferably without the help of lawyers. Keep to the schedule, but be flexible when necessary: sometimes you'll have to sacrifice your time with the child because he has something else that's important for him to do.

- If the friction between you and your ex is too hot, then set the schedule and neutral pick-up spots (such as school), with the help of an involved adult. A full weekend, plus an evening during the week, provides time enough for real contact. The overriding consideration should be the child's welfare, not your convenience.
- Be punctual: pick up and return the child at the agreed times. Your child will feel more secure and you will avoid irritating your ex. Unpunctuality upsets your child, who waits anxiously or suffers the annoyance of your inconvenienced ex.
- Show your ongoing interest in the child. Be involved in your child's school. Include your child in a favorite hobby—or develop a new one—together. Invite his friends over. Encourage him to phone you. One single mother who travels frequently sends her daughter a postcard or letter every day she's away. Gather things of interest to your child during the time you're apart (newspaper clippings, photographs, additions to his collections, etc.). Anything you do like that—such as dropping a note in the mail—lets the child know you're thinking of her even while you're not together. Chat with her, play, *listen*.
- Make it easy for the youngster to love you *and* the other parent. Say nothing negative about your ex to the child. It's such a sad waste of your precious time together to heap verbal abuse on the other parent, not to mention how this hurts the child. Be generous about sharing the child. Avoid asking him questions about your ex's friends. Don't encumber the child with a message you don't have the courage to deliver personally.
- Accept your responsibility as an adult; set reasonable limits on the child's behavior. Your child is not well served if, out of a misplaced sense of guilt or through fear of his disapproval, you allow him to behave wildly. Let him express his feelings about your ex but don't prompt him and don't delight in detrimental descriptions. It's immature to let the child flout limits. It's the child who will suffer by such silly tactics.

WHEN DADDY (OR MUMMY) HAS GONE FOR GOOD

In situations where there is no likelihood of ever seeing the absent parent again, a frank explanation is necessary. Your words, though true, need not be vicious. Don't heap scorn, ridicule and hate on your ex; he or she is an important part of your child's self-image.

Direct your anger in useful channels. Repeat to your child that "daddy (or mummy) didn't leave because of anything you did, or are, or said," (whatever the particular worry of your child), but because you can't live together without fighting and decided it would be best to live apart.

The older the child, the more you can explain. Teen-agers may respond with a surprising empathy. Some children even react with relief if the home atmosphere was very depressing or violent. Honesty is always the best policy in dealing with children, even in these emotionally loaded situations. Just be sure your honesty is really for your child's benefit and not an outpouring of your grievances. Try to put yourself in the child's position.

WHAT THE NEVER-MARRIED MOTHER TELLS HER CHILD

Without exception, the unwed mothers interviewed said they simply tell their children the facts.

The child has done nothing to feel ashamed of. The child will only feel shame if the mother somehow feels condemned herself. The more the mother refuses to accept the scorn of society, and the more matter-of-fact she is about the child's father and why she and he never married, the more the child will grow up with a healthy attitude. As the number of unwed women keeping their babies increases (88 percent in 1977 compared with 30 percent in 1968), the condemnation decreases.

The never-married mother has a couple of years to think through what she is going to say to her child about the father. By the time the child is old enough to talk, most never-married mothers have their attitudes and ideas clear. Answering the child's questions poses little problem. Of course, the more importance you attach to the missing father, the more your child will. So only respond to your child's queries, rather than forcing information on him.

A child will not miss a father she has never known, unless she picks up cues from you or others that she is supposedly lacking something. Samantha, a very capable single mother of a six-year-old girl, says that "too much fuss is generally made about having a father around. We get along fine without one." Emphasize what is important, namely your love for the child and the fact that you decided to give birth and keep her.

An illegitimate child may come up against ridicule. But if the

child has been brought up to have a good self-image, with understanding and compassion and not falsehoods about his origin, prejudice will not hurt him.

A refreshing comment on never-married mothers comes from
Bertha, a divorced mother of two:

Unmarried mothers must surely be remarkable and special human beings.
It cannot be difficult to love a child, any child, but to begin parenthood
without any help takes a brave and strong individual—indeed, a very
loving one, too.

DOES YOUR CHILD NEED
ANOTHER ADULT?

The single father may worry that his child needs a feminine touch; a
single mother may fret over her child's lack of a man around the
house. This missing role-model is really of minor importance. What
is paramount is that the child be loved—by whom is immaterial.

Single mothers who compare their child's lack of a father with the
all-American family are being misled by a myth. Far from being the
rugged hero to their son or daughter, many fathers in coupled families spend little time with their children. A survey in a middle-class
Vancouver neighborhood found that fathers spend an average of
twenty-five minutes a week alone with their sons. Another survey
of twelve countries, including a cross section of North America, revealed that the average father spends no more than twelve minutes
a day with his children.

If your concern is for the child to know how to interact with persons of the sex of the missinr parent later on in life, enroll the child
in some activity that includes adults of that sex. A single woman
who adopted two boys and two girls faced this problem:

I had worried that the kids (girls included) would not have sufficient male
company. But I've been lucky in that I have a lot of friends and many of
my friends are married. The ones I've chosen as godparents are usually
married—to each other—and the men have been very interested in the
children. And I've arranged that the kids do things like go to the Y so they
can meet men instructors there.

Such contact might have helped this man, who recalls an embarrassing moment when he was a child:

It was my first day at the all-boys camp. I was excited at being away from my three sisters and mum for the first time (dad died when I was one and a half). I took a shower, slipped a towel around me just like we did at home, and returned to the dorm. All the other guys began laughing at me. How was I to know boys knot towels around their waists instead of their chests?

One single mother in a metropolitan suburb said she was desperately worried that her son would become a homosexual because of their (mother and son) isolation. She need not have been alarmed. In the first place, the boy had contact with men through her friends, the Boy Scouts and so on. Secondly, nearly every boy in his early years is raised almost entirely by women (mother, day-care teachers, baby-sitters, nursery- and public-school teachers) anyway. Thirdly, what causes homosexuality is unknown, but it does not seem to arise from any one family pattern or sexual experience.

YOUR CHILD'S
SEXUAL IDENTITY

The question of sexual identity is broader than biology or interpersonal relations or images conveyed by television. Do you indicate to your son that men are supposed to be tough and never cry, that men are the bosses and boys don't play with dolls? Are you treating your daughter in ways that tell her that she should be compliant, docile, house-bound and marriage-minded or perhaps career oriented only to secretarial or other traditionally "female" jobs? Does your son learn to take out the garbage while your daughter is responsible for washing dishes? If so, you should not be surprised at the following comment by Louella:

There are men who see something attractive about a woman and would like to say something nice like, "You're very sweet," or "You're so pretty," but all they can blurt out are nasty remarks. Men don't know how to express nice feelings.

We influence our children's concept of their own sexuality in subtle ways. But this is an area in which the child in a single-parent family has an advantage over those in coupled families. The child sees father doing the laundry and cooking. The child receives affection and tenderness, and learns by experience that men can do housework without impairing their masculinity. They can feel and show their feelings and still be men. Similarly, where a woman is the sole parent, the child can see, or at least know that mothers work outside the home, that they can be strong, aggressive, capable, competent and still be women.

Children should be told of the tremendous joy and satisfaction possible in a sexual relationship. They should also be told about venereal disease and rape. Your own feelings about sex are bound to be conveyed to your child. If your experience has not been pleasant (and many single mothers report horrendous moments with men— such events are really violent assault and not sex), think twice before implanting negative ideas in your child. Your child deserves the best information and guidance about sex. This means the emotional as well as the biological facts. The biological facts are readily available in good books; the emotional facts are your responsibility. If you are too shy to discuss these topics, and your ex is unwilling or unavailable, find a healthy-minded person who can.

Do single fathers have a tough time talking with their daughters about sex? Or single mothers with their sons? No—at least it is not an automatically embarrassing situation. One advantage of the characteristic closeness between members of a single-parent family is that a single mother will be able to explain a woman's feelings and attitudes to her son, and a single father can demystify boys' behavior to his daughter. For those single fathers who might find menstruation difficult to discuss, there are free leaflets available in drugstores and from manufacturers of sanitary products. If the single father is going to ask his ex, a woman friend or relative to enlighten his daughter, he should be very sure that the woman has a healthy attitude toward sex. Otherwise he may be handicapping his daughter with fears, false ideas or bitterness. A woman who finds it difficult to use the proper language about menstruation, who calls it "the curse" or other euphemisms, is hardly likely to be instilling sound ideas in the daughter.

INSTILL
SELF-RESPECT

Your child's best defence against fulfilling the assumptions of people who consider him "culturally deprived" and "potentially delinquent" because he comes from a "broken" or one-parent home is a strong feeling of self-worth. How can you help him develop such self-respect? The basis must be in your respect for yourself and for your child. This cannot be faked. It is worth repeating that the never-married mothers interviewed for this book all had healthy attitudes toward themselves. Other kinds of single parents gain respect for themselves and their children through the self-evaluation launched by the shock of separation or loss.

Self-respect is built or destroyed in your child through little things. Really let him make a choice when you've said he can, don't override him at the last moment. Remember that children love to be included in adult activities, even the simple things.

My son threw his arms round me in delight this morning just because I said I'd wait to water the garden until he was back from kindergarten and we could do it together.

Such apparently small gestures are ways of saying, "You are worth my time and interest. You have value as a person."

Because privacy is important in our society, finding some spot, however tiny, where your child can be alone if she wishes is also a way of demonstrating your respect for her. It may be hard in a single-parent home, where space is probably at a premium. But it is imperative if your child has homework and you want her to do well in school. At the very least, let her have exclusive use of the kitchen table for the required time.

To encourage your child's interests is to help safeguard him against whatever makes him feel inferior. No matter what he can do well—play an instrument, collect model cars, grow plants, swim, tell jokes, cook—help him become adept in that one area and you strengthen him for life. Few of us can excel in any of society's vaunted Big B's: Beauty, Brains and Brawn. But no matter how weak your child feels compared to other persons, there will always be that one thing that he does well.

Our power as parents is frightening and heartening at the same time. We have such a strong influence, yet in some ways we have none at all. Most of use can remember the hurt of such an incident as this, related by the now grown-up daughter of a single mother:

One day my sister and I—we were about eleven years old—decided to surprise mother by cleaning up the kitchen. We did a really good job. Everything was spotless. Mother came in, we stood back proudly, waiting for her pleased reaction. All she said was, "You forgot that dust on the cupboard."

An opposite example—building self-respect—was the time Nina praised one of her sons for doing a thorough job vacuuming. Praise develops self-respect in a youngster when it is deserved.

Helping your child develop self-respect and self-confidence means being willing to let him make mistakes. Antoine says he has a terrible habit, which he tries conscientiously to overcome, of frequently saying such things as, "Watch out you don't spill that glass. Careful of the cup. Mind the steps." Such comments might make Antoine's children unsure of themselves, coloring their outlook on life and making them anxious, pessimistic adults; thereby achieving the exact opposite of what Antoine intends. Similarly, the child who has to repeatedly ask for his parent's attention is hardly receiving a lesson in how worthy he is.

The only area in which fear should be bred in children is that of traffic. Our roads are so dangerous (traffic accidents are the second most frequent cause of deaths in North America) that it is a good idea to alert children to the lethal nature of the automobile. There is no room for a child to learn from her mistakes with a car.

SELF-RESPECT
EXERCISE

Take a few moments to complete the Self-respect Chart. You'll gain some insight into your attitude toward your child and how well you are helping to build self-esteem. If you have more than one child, copy out the incomplete sentences for each child after you've replied for the first. Continue on a sheet of paper if there is not enough room. Then,

- If your child is old enough, ask his or her opinions about your answers.
- Have a close adult friend say what he or she thinks about your replies.
- Go over your answers to see what you can do to build your child's self-respect.
- Compare notes with other single parents who have completed their own questionnaires.
- If possible, compare your replies to those of your ex.
- Copy the original sentences leaving the blank portions blank. Make a note on a calendar to fill them in six months from now, without

SELF-RESPECT
CHART

My child's strong points are _____

When my child asks questions about his or her homework _____

To be sure my child has privacy _____

I help my child develop his or her talents by _____

My contacts with my child's teachers _____

When I make an effort to listen to my child _____

When I say "I love you" to my child _____

I help(ed) my child face _____

The last time I praised my child _____

My child smiles when _____

SELF-RESPECT
CHART

When we talk about the child's other parent _____

The most recent occasion I thanked my child was _____

When my child is playing, I _____

My child may never be a champion in school, but _____

Together my child and I do things like _____

I encourage my child to _____

I show affection for my child _____

The kinds of things I praise my child for _____

The tone of voice I use most often with my child _____

In the future, to help my child develop self-respect, I _____ rereading your first set of replies. You won't need to give yourself a reward for progress—you'll only need to look at your child.

DEVELOP
DISCIPLINE

Your child will learn self-discipline from growing up in a framework of imposed discipline. This is using the word in its sense of orderliness, not in the sense of punishment. A highly regarded politician now in his fifties credits his single mother for his drive and pride:

My mother taught me that to achieve great things one must be disciplined. Also she ingrained in me the importance of having basic principles and of being open to people of different languages and backgrounds.

"They know that I'm the boss," is a frequent expression among single parents. To maintain your sanity, especially if you have several children, you know that this is necessary.

I'll make it clear to the children that when I have a guest I want peace to have fun, not to be bothered by them. They have me six nights a week; it's not too much for me to have one night for my own fun without them.

Nina, now a single mother of nine, illustrates the setting of limits coupled with appropriate punishment:

I was alone with six sick children and was pregnant and unwell myself. Three children had measles and three had chicken pox, then they exchanged diseases so I was housebound for two months.
    When they had almost all recovered, they began calling to me to bring them a glass of water—every five or ten minutes. I was almost exhausted physically, and my patience was almost gone as well. I muttered to myself, "If they call me to come upstairs one more time I'll scream and spank every last one of them."
    Well, they did, and I angrily marched upstairs intending to spank them all. When I reached the top of the stairs I saw large red crayoned words on the end wall. At first I was furious, then the message sank in. It read, "My mother is three hundred and sixty-five years old."
    I remember thinking, "You don't know how close to that I feel." Then I sat on the top stair and started to laugh. I needed the laughter to ease the

strain. Then logic caused me to decide who the guilty one was, since most could not write.

The guilty one had to scrub not only that wall, but the other three in that room, and he never wrote on a wall again.

According to Donna, who has been raising two girls, now in their teens, alone since her divorce twelve years ago:

A single parent may worry about being rejected by her child if limits are enforced. Such feelings are particularly likely when the single parent has to deal with teen-agers. Single parents may fall into the danger of not enforcing curfews, for example, for fear the child—who is under a lot of peer pressure—will reject the parent. I've found that a full explanation of *why* I want my daughters in by a certain hour is usually sufficient for them. I wouldn't be fair to myself or to them if I gave into fears of rejection by them.

What should a parent do if the child breaks the rules? A never-married mother with four small children says:

I'm extremely strict. It depends on what rule they break, for example, if they come home late from school they are sent to bed early. You have to lay the grass roots before they are thirteen because after that time you cannot order teen-agers around in the same way. By that time we'll have a sufficient basis of love and common sense that, although at times they will disobey me, at least they will have some understanding that what I'm saying is based on a safety rule or at least on affection.

Some single parents use a points system for the younger child. A certain number of points for specific good behavior and completion of chores. Scoring below a particular number means no allowance that week, or not being allowed out to play or deprivation of something else the child values. Conversely, achievement of a predetermined number of points (or ticks on a wall chart) guarantees certain privileges. Overachievement brings additional rewards. Several single parents report that the system works well, especially with a child who is otherwise difficult to handle. The tasks must be realistic for the child and arranged so that the child competes against himself and not against siblings.

Your child will respond more to rewards for doing the right thing than to punishments for doing the wrong. The reward can be simply praise, encouragement or attention from you—it doesn't have to be cash or cookies. In fact, a child will likely repeat behavior that brings rewards of recognition from the parent. This is the way she learns to talk and to read. It is also the way she learns to sit passively watching television, if that is something we as parents classify as "being good."

Similarly, if a tantrum garners attention but polite behavior does not, the child will learn to have tantrums.

One thing I've realized is that you hope your children will change when they do things you don't like, but it seems *you* usually have to change. Change your approach to the child, that is. Their behavior may be in reaction to something you're doing.

Behavior patterns are set early in life. Arabelle, a never-married single mother, relates the following about her three-year-old son, Mark:

I don't like kids who don't know how to behave. You tell them to do something and they just yell and scream or make faces and embarrass their parents. You take them shopping, you get near the candy or cookies counter, they're reaching out. If you don't give it to them they're going to scream the place down. Mark did that one day. My girl friend was with me. She said, "C'mon, give him a cookie." I said no.

I let him scream. I said no, and that's what I meant. I never buy cookies. I never buy candies. If he's hungry he gets a piece of cheese or fruit. I think cookies and candies are bad for your teeth.

Next time we went to the supermarket, Mark just said, "See the cookies."

It took courage for Arabelle to stick by her convictions while her friend urged her to give in and other shoppers frowned at Mark's screaming. Many a child is either placated or slapped by his parent for fear of disapproval from other adults. We often care more for the opinions of others than we do for the self-image of our child. A single parent should be the child's ally first and foremost. And this goes for the teen-ager in trouble, too. We have an obligation to support our child. Not in a mindless "she's always right" fashion but in an attempt to understand her view. After all, we should know our child better than any teacher, psychologist, police officer or shopper.

Punishments, when really necessary, should be relative to the age of the child.

I'm rather strict with my children by today's standards and mete out punishment according to what is done. They are relegated to their own rooms till fit to be with others. They are grounded if they are fresh or insolent or disobedient about tidying. Spankings are the absolute ultimate—now only for my nine-year-old son—for violent tantrums, or unreasonable, uncontrollable anger at his sister. Most measures come with a good lecture about the rules in this house.

Separated and divorced single parents soon learn not to allow their child to fall into the trap of, "When I'm at Mummy's, she lets me . . . ." or "Daddy said I could stay up till 11:00."

I told my son, that's great. At your dad's, you do what he says. But here, you follow my rules.

The child very quickly picks up what is acceptable *chez* daddy that is forbidden with mummy, and vice versa. Children are remarkably adaptable. They can recognize that their parents are individuals and not an institution. In the words of one boy, who has been shuttling back and forth between his vastly different parents for years:

There are different rules in each house, and all of us kids have had to adjust to them. Mum is definitely stricter than dad.

Although single parents see themselves as being strict, many, especially separated and divorced parents, have wider limits for their children than do coupled families, or even themselves prior to their separation.

In the beginning, I was so beat from suddenly having to do everything myself and all the hassles with lawyers and trying to get a new job that I kind of let things slide a little in the discipline department. But now I've settled into a comfortable routine, and the kids know how much I'll put up with.

Katrina realized the dangers of heaping her frustrations on the children; she devised a useful technique:

I made a promise to myself a few weeks back. Through all the divorce case harassment, I was getting pretty down. A few times I caught myself screaming at the kids just out of my own frustration. They hadn't done anything out of the ordinary.

So I made a promise to myself that every morning when I woke up I would start off with at least one nice thing to say to each kid. And make it a habit. It was like scheduling a lunch hour: scheduling nice words, rather than screaming and yelling.

If you find yourself screaming too much or for inadequate reasons, Jacob, who has a four-year-old son, suggests:

I was getting a sore throat from yelling at Lee. Then I found out by accident (because I *had* a sore throat) that if I whispered, Lee thought that was funny and he made an effort to pay attention. So now I whisper, he listens and I feel calmer.

Nearly every child will respond to fair behavior on your part, coupled with clear reasons for your decisions. To make a child do some manual labor unrelated to his offence as a punishment, is counter-productive. He will learn to look at manual labor as degrading.

FUN
WITH YOUR CHILD

Ruth, a never-married mother and social activist, says a child can be a great inspiration to a single parent:

When I am down, my daughter picks me up right away. She is at such a responsive age (six). She's into so many things, and she's sensing what I'm going through. I'm communicating to a person. She affects me in a really positive way, like just the fun of watching her and listening to her talk. The kind of work I do is very tiring. I come home and she is bubbling about what she learned and she's going to sing me a song and tell me about a new friend—well, that just picks me right up.

Fun with your child can be as simple as a walk around the neighborhood. It's amazing what a child will observe if encouraged. It can also be fun reading to your child and helping him learn to read. Books open a fascinating world. Your child need never be friendless or uninspired if he is taught to appreciate books. Even if a single parent cannot afford to buy books, there is usually a library not too far away.

You have to do what you feel is fun with them. What they like *and* you like. And don't always think you have to go down to their level. Take them along with you in your activities. Bring them *up* to your interests.

THE
ADOLESCENT

Here are the comments of eight adolescent girls, aged fifteen and sixteen, each of whom lives with a mother who is, or was, a single parent. Their frank remarks indicate the emotional turmoil they've been through but also their resilience and common sense.

The girls said that even a very young child can understand the splitting up of her parents and that younger children will adjust faster; a marriage breakup is much more of a shock to a teen-ager. Their advice to children new to single parenthood (via divorce): "Your parents didn't divorce to hurt you. There'll always be a scar, but time will even it out."

If your child is old enough, ask him to make his own list of pros and cons about single parenthood. It could be enlightening for both of you to discuss those and what he thinks of the opinions that follow.

First, the things the girls *don't like* about single parenthood (most of the negative points came from one girl):

RESENTMENT

"My mother never married; sometimes she resents me, she says she regrets not having put me up for adoption, or having me aborted."

"I resent what single parenthood has done to my mother. It's sort of closed her up so there's less communication between us. Also I used to resent my father because he married another woman, and that was like being disloyal to mum, he was replacing her. But now I'm quite close to my father's wife."

JEALOUSY

"A parent may be jealous because the daughter likes the other parent more. And a daughter might be jealous of her mother's boyfriend, if he takes attention away from her."

MOLDING

"Single parents try too hard to mold their children; always telling us not to do such and such, because 'that's just like your father.' "

"I understand why and all that, but my dad shouldn't keep telling me not to walk like that, or say something a certain way, because it's just like your mother. I know when he sees me he sees my mother."

NO SECOND OPINION

"When you're living with your mum, you can't plead with your dad to let you do something mum has forbidden."

LACK OF MONEY

" 'Cause we don't have much money, my mother's always on the lookout for a boyfriend to lean on."

"What I don't like is being nagged at. 'You can't have this, you can't have that.' Why doesn't my mother just tell me how much we've got and we can decide together what we can spend it on."

PSEUDOFATHERS

"What I don't like about boyfriends—and we've been through three of them living with us—is that they like to play father, you know, 'Hey, here's a teen-age girl, it'll be fun to play father, not like changing diapers and stuff . . . .' Well, he has *no right*. He's not my dad. It was different with my stepfather. He was married to mum and I loved him a lot. These guys just like to play at being daddy."

OVERPROTECTION

"My mum's overprotective, maybe because I'm all she's got. She's not so fussy when she's got a boyfriend 'cause then she's worried about two people instead of one."

FEAR

"My mum doesn't date. I think she's scared. She's scared she'll get hurt."

DEPENDENCY

"I'm treated like I'm my mum's mother, not her daughter. She leans on me too much. The responsibility is too heavy."

UNAPPRECIATION

"I help out by doing the shopping for example and soon as I get home, before she sees what I've brought, what does mum say? 'What did you forget?' "

Here's what the girls *like* about single parenthood:

CLOSENESS

"I'm like this with my mother." (Holds up two fingers of one hand as though glued together.)

"It's a bit awkward with my dad, but with mum we're so close I don't have to think of things to say."

"My mother and I are like best friends."

"Single mothers don't keep secrets from you. I like that."

"My mother puts us four kids first, no matter what. Like if she's with her boyfriend and one of us phones, well, she's with us like a shot."

LACK OF MONEY

"I've learned from this: I won't lie to myself that I can't manage and must depend on a man. You just have to cut down on a few things you don't need (such as parties, clothes . . .)."

"You learn not to make the same mistakes as your mother: you have to have a career to fall back on."

"We've been short of money for a good reason: my mum's been working on a degree for eight years. Soon she'll have a Ph.D."

NO JEALOUSY

"Since I've never known my father, I couldn't be more fond of him than my mother, so she's got no reason to be jealous."

TENSIONS RESOLVED

"Tensions are resolved. My mother explained to me: 'Look, I'm suffering, your dad's suffering, it's no good for you, why do you want us to stay together?' I cried a lot, but eventually I understood."

UNDERSTANDING

"Single parents offer more understanding."

"There's more feelings with a single mother. She treats you as a person, with opinions worth listening to."

FAMILY

"My mum made it very clear that the three of us, my brother, her and me, we're a family."

NO SECOND OPINION

"Your mother doesn't have to check everything with your father before giving you a reply about something. It's just between you and her."

INSTRUCTIVE

"You learn from what your mother does; sometimes what not to do. I keep notes on my mother. For instance, she yells over and over at me to do the dishes, but, when I do the dishes without being asked, d'ya think she says anything?"

"I'm like a roommate with my mother. We share all the household tasks. It makes the chores almost fun to do."

RESPECT

"I can't deal with dishonesty so I'm very pleased mum tells me the truth about things. She treats me the way she wants to be treated: like a human being, with rights."

For parents, the hardest part of adolescence is the apparent desire of the child to throw over all the parental values. In one sense, this is simply a phase: the young adult will usually have an underlying core of essentially similar values to his parent. But in another sense —and the one of most consequence—adolescence marks the point at which the human being you have been nurturing is almost ready to step from childhood to adulthood. This means you have to let go, free your daughter to be an adult in her own right. You will be unable to do this effectively and without a terrible amount of emotional suffering unless you have been preparing yourself and your child from early in her life.

Esmerelda, who adopted four children, is optimistic about their adolescence:

There are pessimists around who, whenever I say I'm happy now and I'm glad I've got the children, say, "Wait till they're in their teens and then it will be bad." So I've asked other parents if it really was bad when their children were teens. Generally it seems to me again it's very much your attitude. I think some of my children may be very difficult, one in particular.

But I am a teacher and I've seen a lot of people who were very obnoxious indeed in their teens and I've met them again in their twenties and they were quite different. I made up my mind before I took the children that I would never consider any difficult phase was *it* and was the end. I would assume it could change. And that there wasn't any end to hope or development. Even if the children run away from home and go on to drugs and all the rest of it, I shall obviously be very upset indeed, but I hope I won't decide they'll never come out of it.

Margaret discovered, despite initial misgivings, it is possible to accept the freeing of your offspring:

I found the first year, year and a half, after the separation extremely difficult emotionally. I was very keenly aware of the implications and responsibilities of raising children on my own, especially teen-age boys.

It was a difficult thing for me to do by myself; I felt abandoned. But after a couple of years I felt much more on an even keel.

Now I'm very proud of the job I've done with my kids. See, I still refer to them as kids. But they're men now. Strong, self-reliant men who are kind and thoughtful.

RESOURCES

FOR INFORMATION ON WORK, child care, parent education and other pertinent topics, you may want to get in touch with your local Parent-Teacher Association, Board of Education, Department of Health, Department of Social Services or your local "Y". Check your telephone directory for addresses.

A first step in finding out about colleges, retraining or a myriad other things, is your library's reference librarian. This person's specialty is where to find information. He or she won't have the information, but will tell you where to look, and sometimes even look it up for you. You could find, for example, a listing of all the volunteer groups in your area, a guide to careers or what new books have been written on the subject of single parenting. If there's no public library in your area, contact the nearest university library. Most reference librarians are eager to help: it's their job.

When calling other places for information be persistent: make sure you get through to the right department and to someone who really knows the answers to your questions. Don't get blocked by the receptionist who answers the phone. Call one time and ask for the name of the top official in the department you wish to contact. Then call later and ask for that person by name. You'll be put through to the official's secretary. Frequently, personal secretaries give more information than you'll get from an administrator. Also, if you use their names they'll be more likely to send you information or make sure you get to talk to the boss. Mention this book when you contact the resources listed on the following pages.

FOR
SINGLE PARENTS

Advisory Council on the Status of Women
Suite 1005
151 Sparks Street
Ottawa, Ontario K1P 5R5
Pamphlets about single-parent families, information about women's rights.

Canadian Council on Social Development
55 Parkdale Avenue
Ottawa, Ontario K1Y 1E5
National planning agency; issues statistical studies and policy statements about single-parent families.

Committee for Single Adoptive Parents
P.O. Box 4074
Washington, D.C. 20015
A friendly information service begun in 1973 to help prospective and actual single adoptive parents. Write for advice and price of their new handbook.

National Council of Welfare
Department of National Health and Welfare
Brooke Claxton Building
Tunney's Pasture
Ottawa, Ontario K1A 0K9
For statistics on low-income single parents and addresses of local action groups.

One Parent Families Association of Canada

Ontario and West:	Quebec and East:
Suite 17	P.O. Box 517
2279 Yonge Street	Côte St-Luc Postal Station
Toronto, Ontario M4P 1C7	Montreal, Quebec

Write for information about OPFA, location of your nearest chapter or how to set up a chapter.

Parents Without Partners

Canada: United States:
Suite 13   Suite 1000
205 Yonge Street   7910 Woodmont Avenue
Toronto, Ontario M5B 1N2   Washington, D.C. 20014

Write for information about PWP, location of your nearest chapter or how to set up a chapter.

Single Fathers' Association
180 Sherwood Forest Drive
Markham, Ontario L3P 1R1
Purpose is to minimize the problems of parents separating. (To better reflect their committment to all single parents—both men and women—the name of the Association will be changed.)

Superintendent of Documents
Government Printing Office
Washington, D.C. 20402
Write for leaflets and books, many free, in your areas of interest: child care, budgeting, day care, women and work, etc.

DAY CARE AND
PLAY GROUPS

American Academy of Pediatrics
P.O. Box 1034
Evanston, Illinois 60204
Write for *Recommendations for Day Care Centers for Infants and Children.*

Child Care Resource Center
187 Hampshire Street
Cambridge, Massachusetts 02139
Write for its list of publications, including *How to Select a Child Care Center.*

Child Welfare League of America
44 East 23rd Street
New York, New York 10010
Write for general information and publications.

National Assocation for Child Development and Education
500 12 Street, SW.
Washington, D.C. 20024
Send for information regarding day care centers.

National Day Care Information Centre
Health and Welfare Canada
Brooke Claxton Building
Tunney's Pasture
Ottawa, Ontario K1A 1B5
Provides information on day care centers. Write for information and/or brochures and pamphlets.

The Mothers' Center
United Methodist Church
Old Country Road at Nelson Avenue
Hicksville, New York 11801
Write for information about setting up a play group with a difference. (Include a self-addressed, stamped envelope.)

EDUCATION AND EMPLOYMENT

American Association of University Women
2401 Virginia Avenue NW.
Washington, D.C. 20037
The AAUW acts as a clearinghouse for information regarding women's educational opportunities. Write for its fact sheets.

Association of Universities and Colleges
The Library
151 Slater Street
Ottawa, Ontario K1P 5N1
Write to find out where to get a copy of the *Directory of University Correspondence Courses* put out by the Canadian Association for University Continuing Education.

Canada Employment and Immigration Commission
Coordinator, Women's Employment
Second Floor
Vanier Building
222 Nepean Street
Ottawa, Ontario
For details on affirmative action programs; also where to go in your province.

Catalyst
14 East 60th Street
New York, New York 10022
This organization aids women all over the country with its career planning, job placement and educational advisory services. It also prepares useful publications, such as *Your Job Campaign*. Write for complete information.

Department of Industry, Trade and Commerce
Ottawa, Ontario K1A 0H5
Write for the *Doing Business in Canada* series, a free mini-library of clearly written booklets on all aspects of starting your own business.

Displaced Homemakers
Business and Professional Women's Foundation
2012 Massachusetts Avenue NW.
Washington, D.C. 20036
Many states have passed measures to give help to displaced homemakers, women over thirty-five who, through divorce, separation, widowhood or other crises in midlife, have been forced into the labor market with little training. The Washington address is a clearinghouse for information and referral to local centers which offer counseling and job training programs.

Federal Business Development Bank
Head Office
901 Victoria Square
Montreal, Quebec H2Z 1R1
Provides an inquiry and referral service about government and other assistance programs for small businesses. Write for *Minding Your Own Business,* a series of booklets, and *Small Business News,* a quarterly news bulletin.

International Association of Counseling Services
1607 New Hampshire Avenue NW.
Washington, D.C. 20009
Its *Directory of Approved Counseling Agencies* lists types of services, hours and charges for counselors in the United States and Canada.

Midol Career Booklet
P.O. Box 3899
Rochester, New York 14621
Write for *Where the Jobs Are,* a guide for women on career opportunities, including pay scales and the types of training needed. Free.

Montreal Household Worker Association
445 St. Francois Xavier
Montreal, Quebec H3N 2G8
A union-like group for domestic workers.

National Association of Trade and Technical Schools
2021 K Street, NW.
Washington, D.C. 20006
Write for their *Handbook of Trade and Technical Careers,* which can provide a helpful roundup of accredited private and technical schools, as well as explanations of the jobs available in various fields. Free.

National Association of Women in Construction
2800 West Lancaster Avenue
Fort Worth, Texas 76107
Write for free booklet *"Considering a career in construction."*

National Committee on Household Employment
500 East 62nd Street
New York, New York 10012
Trying to get a better deal for domestic workers: may know of a group near you.

National Organization for Women (NOW)
Suite 1615
5 S. Wabash
Chicago, Illinois 60603

Its eight hundred local chapters provide employment seminars, legal advice and referral services.

The Project on the Status and Education of Women
Association of American Colleges
1818 R Street NW.
Washington, D.C. 20009
Publishes *Financial Aid: A Partial List of Resources for Women,* an extensive listing of scholarship programs, general and specialized, including a number directed to mature women or returning students. Includes extensive resource bibliography. Free.

Rank and File
2002 Hotel de Ville
Montreal, Quebec H2X 3B2
Regarding rights of nonunionized workers.

Regional Learning Service
405 Oak Street
Syracuse, New York 13203
Publishes *Women's Career Handbook,* which presents information gathered from participants in a local women's career workshop (plus reference sources) on specific jobs, education or training required, approximate cost of education, career outlook, salary range, skills and duties involved. Free.

The Women's Bureau
Rights and Employment Branch
Labour Canada
Ottawa, Ontario K1A 0J2
Write for free literature about careers.

United States Department of Health and Human Services
Office of Bureau of Higher Education
40 Maryland Avenue SW.
Washington, D.C. 20202
Write for *A Selected List of Post-secondary Education Opportunities for Minorities and Women.*

United States Department of Labor Employment and Training Administration
Washington, D.C. 20213
Write for *Merchandising Your Job Talents,* a guide to self-appraisal, preparing a resume and letter of application and job-interview techniques. Free.

Women's Bureau
Canadian Labor Congress
2841 Riverside Drive
Ottawa, Ontario K1V 8X7
For information and leaflets on women in unions and in the workplace.

Women's Bureau
United States Department of Labor
14th Street and Constitution Avenue NW.
Washington, D.C. 20210
Write for a list of leaflets; some are free, such as *Get Credit for What You Know.*

HEALTH

Federal Department of Health and Welfare
Health Services and Promotion Branch
8th floor, Journal Building
365 Laurier Avenue W.
Ottawa, Ontario K1A 1B6
Numerous leaflets on nutrition, teens and drugs, children, etc. Ask for list.

Montreal Diet Dispensary
2182 Lincoln Avenue
Montreal, Quebec H3H 1J3
For the latest information about nutrition, especially for pregnant women but also relevant to any single-parent family.

Nutrition Information Service
Room 1955
Learning Resources Centre
Ryerson Polytechnical Institute
50 Gould Street
Toronto, Ontario M5G 1E8
Offers a clearinghouse for information on nutrition research.

MONEY

Bureau of Consumer Protection
Washington, D.C.
Credit problems and false advertising hot line. Call 202-523-3727.

Consumer Information Center
Pueblo, Colorado 81009
For a free, quarterly catalog of two hundred or so selected federal publications (free or cheap) dealing with many subjects of interest to single parents, write for *The Consumer Information Catalog.*

Energy, Mines and Resources Canada
Enersave Questionnaire
P.O. Box 4510, Station E
Ottawa, Ontario K1S 5K3
Write for the *Enersave Questionnaire* on saving energy and money.

Energy, Mines and Resources Canada
P.O. Box 3500, Station C
Ottawa, Ontario K1Y 4G1
Write for the *New Motorist's Guide,* on the purchase, operation and maintenance of a car with an eye to saving energy and money. Free, including a copy of the *Fuel Consumption Guide.*

Federal Reserve System
The Board of Governors
Washington, D.C. 20551
Write for *Consumer Handbook to Credit Protection Laws.*

Office of Consumer Affairs
Department of Energy
Washington, D.C. 20585
Write for *Winter Survival,* a booklet on energy-efficient living through winter.

United States Department of Energy
Technical Information Center
P.O. Box 62
Oak Ridge, Tennessee 37830
Write for *Tips for Energy Savers* on how to curb energy use to save money and resources. Free.

FAMILY AND
CHILDHOOD PROBLEMS

American Association of Marriage and Family Counselors, Inc.
225 Yale Avenue
Claremont, California 91711
Write for a list of counselors in your area.

Canadian Mental Health Association
2160 Yonge Street
Toronto, Ontario M4S 2Z3
Ten pamphlets on "Feelings and Your Child" available for 25¢.

Contact Teleministries
Chapters in ninety cities in the United States. Provides a twenty-four-hour counseling hot line. Check phone book or call the national headquarters: 717-652-3410.

Neurotics Anonymous
Washington, D.C.
Counseling hot line. Check phone book or call 202-628-4379.

Parents Anonymous
Child abuse hot line, open every day. Call 800-421-0353 (California, 800-352-0386).

FOR AND
ABOUT CHILDREN

Big Brothers-Big Sisters of America
220 Suburban Station Building
Philadelphia, Pennsylvania 19103

Big Brothers of Canada
P.O. Box 758
Burlington, Ontario L7R 3Y7

Boys' and Girls' Clubs of Canada
620 Wilson Avenue
Downsview, Ontario M3K 1Z3

Boys' Club of America
771 1st Avenue
New York, New York 10017

Children of Gays
Apt 11D
430 East Sixth Street
New York, New York 10009

Children's Defense Fund
For information on national issues and referal to the proper government agency, call 800-424-9602.

Child Study Association of America
Wel-Met, Inc.
50 Madison Avenue
New York, New York 10010
Write for a list of their publications giving advice on various childhood stress situations, such as *What to Tell Your Child about Sex*
and *Helping Your Child Understand Death.*

Council on Family Health
633 Third Avenue
New York, New York 10017
Write for *The Care and Safety of Young Children.* Includes such
tips as storing medicine properly and rules for fire safety. Free.

House of Representatives
(Name of your Representative)
Washington, D.C. 30515
Infant Care is one of several great booklets available. Get your
Representative's name from your library or newspaper office.

National Runaway Switchboard
Runaway twenty-four hour hot line. Call 800-621-4000 (Illinois,
800-393-3352).

Operation Peace of Mind
Runaway twenty-four hour hot line. Call 800-231-6946 (Texas,
800-392-3352).

Society for Emotionally Disturbed Children
1622 Sherbrooke W.
Montreal, Quebec H3H 1C9

MISCELLANEOUS

Children's Rights, Inc.
Washington, D.C.
Kidnapping by noncustodial parent hot line. Call 202-462-7573.

National Legal Aid and Defender Association
Check phone book for local listing or call 202-452-0620.

Single Booklovers
Box AE
Swarthmore, Pennsylvania
Write for details of fees and procedures.

**HUD Office of Fair Housing & Equal Opportunity Discrimination
Hotline**
Provides basic legal information and details on how to file a com-
plaint. Call 800-424-8590.

Single mothers who are sexually harrassed at work can contact one
of these organizations for a referral to a support group in their area:

Working Women's Institute
593 Park Avenue
New York, New York 10021
212-838-4420

Alliance Against Sexual Coercion
P.O. Box 1
Cambridge, Massachusetts 02139
617-482-0329

Women for Racial and Economic Equality (WREE)
130 East 16th Street
New York, New York 10003
212-473-6111
WREE concentrates on helping women in blue-collar jobs.

SUGGESTIONS FOR FURTHER READING

FOR
CHILDREN

Always read a child's book before buying it. Tastes and reading levels vary a great deal. Many good books are available only in libraries (*Mushy Eggs,* for example, which is about separated parents who both work). New books for children in single-parent families are coming out frequently. Check with your reference librarian or bookstore for titles that might suit your family.

Berger, Terry. *How Does It Feel When Your Parents Get Divorced?* New York: Julian Messner (Simon and Schuster), 1977. Plain talk brought to life with photographs designed to help the child face his or her feelings. For children about six to eleven.

Blume, Judy. *It's Not the End of the World.* New York: Bantam Books, 1977. A warm, fictional story for children in grades 4 to 6. A girl tries in vain to get her divorced parents back together.

Crawford, Sue Heffernan. *Minoo's Family.* Toronto: Before We Are Six, 1976. A little girl's feelings of loneliness, anger and confusion as her parents separate.

Gardner, Richard A. *Boys' and Girls' Book about One-Parent Families.* New York: Putnam, 1978. Gardner has a similar book on divorce. Question and answer format covers all the ground but sounds somewhat forced.

Geoffroy, Bernice. *Irene's Idea.* Toronto: Before We Are Six, 1975. How a fatherless child copes with Father's Day at school.

Grollman, Earl A. *Talking About Divorce.* Boston: Beacon Press, 1975. Similar to Berger's book but with sketches. Draws out the child-reader's feelings while reinforcing that both parents still love him or her.

Mark, Susan E. *"Please, Michael, That's My Daddy's Chair".* Toronto: Before We Are Six, 1976. A single mother of three brings male friends home.

Schick, Eleanor. *Home Alone.* New York: Dial Press, 1980. A warm, realistic story about Andy, who comes home to an empty house. For children four to eight.

FOR ADULTS

Although many of the books and other materials which are relevant to the single parent are ostensibly aimed at women only, most are ideal for men as well as women. Also, don't take a book as sacred simply because it's in print; make up your own mind about what it suggests.

BOOKS

Berman, Eleanor. *Re-entering: Successful Back-to-Work Strategies for Women Seeking a Fresh Start.* New York: Crown Publishers, 1980. An inspiring, detailed practical volume for the woman returning to the work force after being home for several years. Deals mostly with women who have some college education, although there is lots of advice for others, too.

Bolles, Richard. *What Color is Your Parachute?* Berkely: Ten Speed Press, 1980. Updated every year, this is fast becoming the classic how-to-get-the-job-you- really-want guide.

Endicott, Fran, and Thomas, Barb. *The City Kids' Book.* Toronto: Ontario Institute for Studies in Education, 1979. A book that presents the reality of working-class and immigrant and single-parent families in cities. Available for $7 from the Institute (252 Bloor St. W., Toronto, Ontario M5S 1V6).

Goldberg, Herb, Ph.D. *The New Male: From Macho to Sensitive but Still All Male.* New York: Signet, 1980. How a man can free himself from hurtful stereotypes: learn, for example, to spot a woman putting him in a "no-win" situation and how to stop worrying about failure in bed or boardroom.

Greenleaf, Barbara Kaye, and Schaffer, Lewis A., M.D. *Help: A Handbook for Working Mothers.* New York: Berkley Publishing Corporation, 1980. Packed with detailed advice on juggling home and children.

Hope, Karol, and Young, Nancy. *Momma: The Source Book for Single Mothers.* New York: New American Library, 1976. The earliest worthwhile book for single mothers. Some of the sources are now dated, but the book is worth reading for the courageous stories and vital viewpoint alone.

King, Lyn. *What Every Woman Should Know About Marriage, Separation and Divorce.* Toronto: James Lorimer, 1980. Clear, specific legal information for every Canadian province except Quebec.

Knight, Bryan, and Long, Doug. *The Laughter Book,* Toronto: Musson Books, 1979. How to develop your sense of humor, size others up by the way they laugh, use laughter to gain friends, promotion, romance.

Kunin, Richard A., M.D. *Mega-Nutrition: The New Prescription for Maximum Health, Energy and Longevity.* New York: McGraw-Hill Book Company, 1980. How to use food and vitamins to overcome anxiety, depression, hyperactivity. An easy-to-read volume with lots of case histories, particularly on the dangers of sugar. Well worth the steep price.

Leslie, Mary, and Seltz, David D. *New Businesses Women Can Start and Successfully Operate.* New York: Barnes and Noble Books, 1979. Written rather cutely, but full of plausible suggestions for small businesses you might begin. Also contains short accounts of successful businesses that grew large.

Maxwell, Rhonda. *Supershopping and You: Rhonda Maxwell's Canadian Guide to Saving up to 40% on Your Annual Grocery Bill.* Toronto: Penguin Books, 1980. A slim volume that could fatten your pocketbook.

Mouat, Lucia. *Back to Business; A Woman's Guide to Reentering the Job Market.* New York: Signet Books, 1980. W. Willard Witz, former United States Secretary of Labor, says this book can double a woman's chances.

Norris, Gloria, and Miller, Jo Ann. *The Working Mother's Complete Handbook.* New York: Dutton, 1979. A forthright, helpful guide to handling home, work and children.

Perkins, Gail, and Rhoades, Judith. *The Women's Financial Survival Handbook.* New York: Plume Books (New American Library), 1980. Everything that men are presumed to know already: about credit, banking, business, budgeting, assets, providing for old age, etc.

Pomroy, Martha. *What Every Woman Needs To Know About the Law.* New York: Doubleday, 1980. Exactly.

Roman, Mel, and Haddad, William. *The Disposable Parent: The Case for Joint Custody.* New York: Penguin Books, 1979. Despite the weird title and some heavy writing, this is the primer for joint custody. The book marshals all the arguments and presents a fascinating historical account of society's various attitudes toward children and custody.

Ross, Kathleen Gallagher. *Good Day Care: Getting It, Keeping It, Fighting For It.* Toronto: Women's Press, 1978. A primer on the value of day care and how to establish good facilities.

Samtur, Susan J., and Tuleja, Tad. *Cashing In at the Checkout.* New York: Warner Books, 1980. Even if you're not coupon crazy, you'll learn many useful tips to cut your food bills.

Sarshik, Steven and Szykitka, Walter. *Without a Lawyer.* New York: Plume Books, 1980. A step-by-step guide to many legal procedures, including divorce, that you can carry out yourself without a lawyer.

Schaefer, Charles E. *How To Influence Your Children*. Toronto: Van Nostrand Reinhold, 1978. A handbook of parenting skills; how to raise self-confident children. Concludes with summaries of major theories of child development.

Snyder, J. Christopher, and Anderson, Brian E. *It's Your Money, The Complete Canadian Guide to Personal Financial Planning*. Toronto: Methuen Publications, 1979. How to handle taxes, investments, savings, estate planning; charts and questionnaires cover everything.

Townson, Monica, and Stapenhurst, Frederick. *The Canadian Women's Guide to Money*. Toronto: McGraw-Hill Ryerson, 1979. Short but thorough.

MAGAZINES

Essence: The Magazine for Today's Black Woman. Packed with solid, inspiring information and stories. Aimed at all black women but usually contains down-to-earth facts especially helpful to single mothers. On your newsstand or write P.O. Box 2989, Boulder, Colorado 80302.

McCall's Working Mother: Frequently has articles specifically for single mothers. Lots of generally useful information. On your newsstand or write P.O. Box 10609, Des Moines, Iowa 50336.

New Woman: Mostly excerpts from self-help books; very uplifting. On your newsstand or write: P.C. Drawer 189, Palm Beach, Florida 33480.

Protect Yourself: An informative and useful monthly magazine for the Quebec consumer. Free from l'Office de la protection du consommateur, Edifice Place Haute-Ville, 700 St-Cyrille Blvd. E., 15th floor, Quebec G1R 5A9.

Working Woman: Full of tips on managing home, work and children at the same time. Budget tips, cooking hints, etc. On your newsstand or write: P.O. Box 10130, Des Moines, Iowa 50349 for current price.

ENJOYING SINGLE
PARENTHOOD QUESTIONNAIRE

Much of the material in this book was gathered from the responses of single parents to an extensive questionnaire. Some of the questions are reprinted below. If you wish to answer them, or if you have suggestions for improving *Enjoying Single Parenthood,* write to

Bryan M. Knight
Chess Nut Bookshop
4866 Sherbrooke St. W.
Westmount, Quebec H3Z 1H1

- Name, address, phone, sex, marital status; children, sexes and ages.
- What do you consider the three best things about being a single parent?
- What and how do you tell your children about the missing parent?
- What methods have you found most successful in coping with loneliness?
- What specific things do you do to stretch your income?
- How do you deal with feelings of guilt?
- How do you handle your own sexual needs?
- How do you handle discrimination against single parents in housing or jobs?
- Describe your feelings about being a single parent.
- If you are employed outside the home, how do you manage the house and children?
- How much time do you spend with your children? What kinds of things do you do?
- What tips do you have, as a single parent, about looking after babies, young children, teenagers?
- How do you manage to have time for yourself?
- What would you like to know about other single parents?
- What do you think about children working around the house?
- What do you do if your children seem to be overly seeking attention from other people (especially those of the opposite sex)?

- How do you cope when you get sick?
- How do you react to people offering you unsolicited advice?
- What ideas would you like your children to have about marriage?
- How involved are you and/or the children with the other parent (both in terms of feeling and time)? With other family members on either side?
- Describe professional help you have had.
- Describe your family's (your parents, siblings) attitudes to your single parenthood.
- How do you handle differences of opinion with your family?
- What are your thoughts on getting married (or remarried)?
- What do your children feel about being part of a single parent family? (If possible, ask them to write something frank themselves.)
- How do you find reliable babysitters?
- What do you consider the major factors in child-raising within a single parent family?
- How do you meet people to date?
- Describe an incident or two which made "it all seem worthwhile."
- What are the advantages for a child growing up in a single parent family?
- When things seem too tough to live through, where do you find the strength to continue?
- What have you learned about yourself as a result of being or becoming a single parent?
- What are your opinions about never-married single parents?
- Describe your involvement in actions to help single parents (e.g., attempts to get government aid for day care centers).
- List practical hints, no matter how obvious to you, that make housekeeping, cooking, shopping, childcare, easier.
- Describe your living arrangements (are you sharing with other single parents, for example?).
- What is your opinion about having sexual relations in your home?
- What do you think are the possibilities, advantages and disadvantages of dating other single parents? Single non-parents?
- What laws or attitudes or situations need changing for the benefit of single parents?
- Do you have any other comments, ideas, suggestions? Your children are welcome to add their own views (uncensored, please).

INDEX

Adolescents, 50, 53, 110, 113, 127
143-47
Adoptive single parent, 5-7
Advantages of single parenthood,
1, 2, 8, 10-12
Aid to Families with Dependent
Children (AFDC). See Welfare
Alimony. See Support payments
Anger
of child, 119
toward child, 23
exercise, 23, 24-25
overcoming, 20, 22-23, 117, 118
Anxiety, 31, 85, 116

Babysitters, 50-51
Baking soda, use of, 66
Block parents, 51
Boys and Girls Clubs, 28, 52
Budgeting. See Finances

Child abuse, 23
Children from single-parent families
after-school arrangements for,
48, 51-52
allowances for, 122
discipline of, 138-42
discussion with, about
absence of other parent, 129-30
being from a single-parent
family, 79-80
illegitimacy, 130-31
parent's dating, 110-12
relationship with ex-partner, 119
empathy exercise, 13-14
fun with, 12, 142-43
groups for, 78, 119
illegitimate, 74, 117, 130-31
independence of, encouraging,
121-22
jobs for, 123
only, 120-21
and school, 79-80
self-respect of, 133-34
exercise, 135, 136-37
sexual identity of, 132-33

Church groups, help from, 32
Clothing, saving money on, 61
Cooperative living, 39-40, 49, 69
Counselors (Psychiatrists,
Psychologists, Social Workers),
29, 31-32
how to find, 31, 41
Credit. See also Finances
discrimination when obtaining, 83
Equal Credit Opportunity Act, 84
how to obtain, 83-84
Custody of children, 73, 74, 76, 120
after death of parent, 74
joint, 7, 73, 126-28
mediation to decide, 74

open, 7
parent without, 128-29

Dating, 101-03. See also Meeting
people; Sex
and child, 111-12, 114-15
patterns
denial, 105
non-fit, 103-04
unhealthy, 104-05
relationship exercise, 105, 107-09
Daughter and single father, 9-10, 12,
27, 125, 131, 133
Day care, 49, 90
family, 91
how to find, 92
parent-run, 91-92
private, 92
shortage of, 90-91
Depression, overcoming, 16-17. See
also Help
Diet. See Food
Discipline of children, 138-42
Discrimination. See Prejudice
Divorced single parents, 2, 4, 33, 34,
73, 106
children of, 11, 117
Drugs, 17 31

Emotions, overcoming destructive,
17, 20
Employment
discrimination against single
parents seeking, 69-72
of men, 8
outside the home, 47-48
arrangements for children,
48, 51-52
part-time, 48
self-, 48, 71
training for, 46-47, 71
of women, 7, 47, 69-70, 90
Equal Credit Opportunity Act, 84
Exercises
anger, 23, 24-25
children
empathy, 13-14
self respect of, 135, 136-37
dating, relationship, 105, 107-09
ex-partner, 20, 21-22
guilt, 16, 18-19
loneliness, overcoming, 36-37
self development, 29, 30
time management, 55, 56
Ex-partner, 15, 20, 76
anger toward, overcoming, 17, 20,
117-19
befriending, 22
and child, 119, 125, 128-29
dating people similar to, 103
exercise, 20, 21-22
sex with, 22

Extended family, 38

Faith, 32
Family court, 73
Father, single
  attitudes toward, 3, 8, 80
  custody by, 7, 73
  and dating, 99, 100, 102
  and daughter, 9-10, 12, 27, 125, 133
  employment of, 8-9
  and finances, 57
  and groups for single parents, 42
  and housework, 64-65
  and housing, 68
  and schools, 78
  and sex, 94-95
  and sitters, 50-51
  and welfare, 8, 85

Finances, 57
  allowances for children, 122
    credit, 83-84
    cutting expenses, 57-63
      on clothing, 61
      on food, 57, 59-60
      on laundry, 61
      on toys, 61
    debt, 59
Food
  proper diet, importance of, 64, 89
  saving money on, 57, 59-60, 89
  saving time preparing, 63, 64
Friends
  child's need for adult, 114-15
  losing, 34, 82, 99
  making and contacting, 34-35, 99-100
  male, 99-103
  natural and professional, 31
Funeral, arranging, 74, 75

Grandparents, 38, 82
Grief
  helping child overcome, 116
  overcoming, 17, 20
Groups. See also Organizations for single parents
  for children of single parents, 78, 119
  for single mothers, 42-43, 89
  for single parents, 42
Guilt
  exercise, 16, 18-19
  helping child overcome, 117
  overcoming, 13-16, 119

Help
  emotional
    from church groups, 32
    from counselors, 29, 31-32

through faith, 32
    from helping others, 27-28
    from single parent organizations and groups, 40-43
  with finances, 59
  with legal matters, 74
Homosexuality, 132
  homosexual single parents, 98
Housework, 57, 64-66
  children helping with, 122-23
Housing
  discrimination against single parents looking for, 67-69
  mortgages, 67-68
  moving to new accommodation, 44-45, 87
Human Rights Commission, 70
Humor, developing a sense of, 27

Illegitimate children, 74, 117, 130-31
Information, how to get, 148

Jobs. See Employment

Language, biases of, 81-82
Laundry, saving money on, 61, 65
Lawyers. See Legal system
Legal aid, 75-76
Legal system, 4, 72, 73, 74. See also Custody
  adversary system, 72, 74
  lawyers, 72, 74, 76-78
    how to find, 75-76
  legal aid, 75-76
  prejudice against single parents in, 72-73
Loneliness
  overcoming, 33-36, 38
    cooperative living, 39-40
    enjoying solitude, 36
    exercise, 36-37
    extended family, 38
    single-parent groups, 42-43
    single-parent organizations, 40-42
Love
  of child for parent, 10-11
  toward child, 1, 9, 23, 82, 99, 111, 116, 119, 126
  for ex, 22
  need for, 97

Media
  fighting prejudice in, 80-81
  portrayal of single parents in, 1, 80
Meeting people of the opposite sex, 99-100. See also Dating; Sex
  through newspaper "personals", 100
  through a party, 99-100
  through single-parent

organizations, 40-41, 99
Money, controlling. See Finances
Montreal Diet Dispensary, 89
Mothers Organizing Mothers, 86
Mothers, single
    attitudes toward, 3, 80-81, 85
    and dating, 100
    employment of, 47, 69-72, 90
    and finances, 83-84
    groups for, 42-43, 89
    and housing, 67-68
    and legal system, 73
    never-married, 15-16, 130-31
    return to school of, 47
    and sex, 96, 97, 98, 106, 113
    and son, 110, 132, 133
    and welfare, 85-86, 87-90
Moving to new accommodation,
    44-45, 87

Never-married single parents, 5
    adoptive, 5-7
    single mothers, 15-16
        children of, 130-31

One Parent Families Association,
    41-42, 99
Organizations for single parents,
    40-42

Parents, single. See Single parents
Parents Without Partners, 41, 99
Past, freeing yourself from, 17, 20
Play groups, 49-50
Prejudice and discrimination against
        single parents, fighting
    credit, 83-84
    employment, 69-72
    housing, 67-69
    language, 81-82
    legal system, 72-78
    media, 80-81
    school, 78-80
    social situations, 82
    welfare, 85-90
Preschoolers, 49, 66

Relaxation, importance of, 52
Rent-A-Mum, 51
Role models, lack of, 131-32

School
    arrangements for child after,
        48, 51-52
    discrimination in, 78-79
    single parent returning to, 46-47, 89
Self-development, 26, 28, 29, 36, 45
    exercise, 29, 30
Selfishness, responsible, 45
Self-respect, instilling in child,
    133-35
Separated single parents, 4, 82

children of, 117
Sex, 94, 96-97. See also Dating;
        Meeting people
    abstinence from, 95
    casual, 101-02
    with ex-partner, 22
    homosexuality, 98, 132
    masturbation, 96
    sexual identity of children, 132-33
    single fathers and, 94-95, 98
    single mothers and, 96, 97, 98,
        106, 113
    sleep-over dates, 106, 110-11
Sexual stereotypes, 3, 8, 80, 132-33
Shuttle single parent, 125-26, 128-29
Single parent. See also Father, single;
        Mother, single
    adoptive, 5-7
    divorced, 2, 4, 33, 34, 73, 106
    never-married, 15-16
    separated, 4, 82, 117
    widowed, 5, 33, 117
Single parenthood, advantages of
    for child, 1, 10
    for parent, 1, 2, 3, 10-12
Sitters, 50-51
Social aid. See Welfare
Social slights, how to overcome, 82
Solitude, savoring, 37
Son and single mother, 22, 110, 118,
    121, 131, 133
State Equal Employment
    Opportunity Commission, 70
Stereotypes, sexual, 3, 8, 132-33
Support payments, 73, 84, 87. See
    also Finances

Tape recorder, use by single parent,
    53-54
Teenagers. See Adolescents
Therapy, 29, 31
    groups, 42
Time
    finding time for yourself, 49-50
    planning time, 54
    quality time with child, 124
    saving time, 53, 63
    time management exercise, 55, 56
Toys, saving money on, 61

Welfare
    discrimination against single
        fathers applying for, 8, 85-86
    how to obtain, 86-87
    living on, 87-90
    rights groups, 86
Widowed single parents, 5, 33
    children of, 117
Will, preparing a, 74
Wives, battered, 104
Working outside the home. See
    Employment